This is not just a book about "middle age." It's a book about life—how to live more fully, more richly, more purposefully than ever before! Accordingly, it's not just for people who are already into "the second half of life." We believe *The Best Half of Life* can also be read profitably by young adults—men and women in their twenties and early thirties. It is during these years that lifestyles are forged, values formulated, families started, careers shaped. Ray and Anne Ortlund's wise and helpful advice can be of special value in looking ahead and determining the direction of the years to come.

So whether you are twenty-five, or forty, or sixty-five, or ninety—enjoy this book! We suspect that reading it may mark the beginning of a whole new life for you—a life filled with creativity, enthusiasm, excitement, and the unmistakable sense of the presence of God.

—The Publisher

Other Books by Ray Ortlund

Lord, Make My Life a Miracle
Lord, Make My Life Count
Reach for Life
Intersections: With Christ at the
    Crossroads of Life
Circle of Strength

Other Books by Anne Ortlund

Up with Worship
Disciplines of the Beautiful Woman
Love Me with Tough Love

RAY & ANNE ORTLUND

The Best Half of Life

WORD BOOKS
PUBLISHER
WACO, TEXAS

ISBN 0-8499-2924-5
Library of Congress Catalog Card Number 77-21582

First Paperback Printing: September 1980
Second Paperback Printing: September 1984

Contents

Prologue

Friend, there's someone coming down the road toward you. Take a look. It's you, 25 years from now.

Perhaps you've never before looked at your future self. Have you? If you're now anywhere from 35 to 50, this Future You walking toward you has slowed down somewhat—but it's you, all right.

Well, what do you think? Does this person walking toward you look sharper than you, and better, and wiser, and godlier, and more fun—just an all-around general improvement?

The two of us are writing this book as a project launched from our fiftieth birthdays. (We're just a few months apart in age.) It's to say the things we wish we'd been told between ages 35 and 50, a book to tell you "how to," a book for fun, a book to lead you to God as you contemplate living the second half of life.

You mustn't waste another day waiting to get on with it. "Dear Abby" says the only thing that comes to those who wait is grey hair.

Life is so precious, and each day is important. Friend, how do you know you're laying the right groundwork for what's ahead?

That Future You is coming down the road now. Let's talk.

1.

Today Is the First Day of the Rest of Your Life

Shut your eyes for a moment, and imagine the next 25 years of your life. What could you believe God for in that precious, irreplaceable period?

The two of us were recently teaching a workshop together on the middle years, and we were curious how perhaps a hundred dedicated Christian workers would answer that question. So we asked them to write down in one sentence how they envisioned their lives in the next 25 years. Sadly, these active Christian workers had no idea where they were going. We suspect many Christians are the same: like sheep, going along with their heads down from one tuft of grass to the next, with no sense of direction or plan.

"How do you envision your lives?"

"Sorry, no projections" ("All we like sheep . . .").

"I can only take it one day at a time," (one tuft of grass after another . . .).

"Accomplishing more" (nibble, nibble . . .).

"I probably don't have that long to wait for glory."

"No goals."

The rest of the responses were similar. Now, these answers reveal such need that we can hardly wait to get this book written and into print. By the time a Christian is well launched into adulthood, he ought to have a clear vision of where he's been, where he is now, and where (God willing) he's going. How else can he know what to eliminate and what to concentrate on in order to stay on target?

Long ago Lee Downing, who was a missionary in Africa from 1901 to 1942 under the Africa Inland Mission, put it this way:

"Before a stone of a foundation is laid, the architect has thought through the prepared detailed specifications regarding the shape and size of the building, and of every piece of material entering into its construction. God's plan for your life is not less definite."[1]

When you look at the foundations of a building even before it rises out of the ground, you can pretty much guess whether it's going to be a skyscraper or a ranch-type house. And by the time it's half completed, you shouldn't find it hard at all to envision how the second half will look.

Here you are, maybe between 35 and 50. You know what your talents are by now, your skills; what your preparation has been; who the people are around you who may or may not be involved in the completion of your "house." And reason tells you that you can set specific goals to finish life gloriously.

And beyond reason, faith says so. God says so.

Ephesians 2:10 declares you're "created in Christ Jesus for good works, which God prepared beforehand, that [you] should walk in them" (*NASB*).

"Be . . . not unwise," God warns you in Ephesians 5:17, "but understanding what the will of the Lord is" (*KJV*).

Better yet, "that you may be filled with the knowledge of His will,"[2] moving confidently into your own vision of God's glorious future for you, knowing what to do and what not to do to help you get there.

Where do you learn His plan for you? "Counsel is mine,"[3] says the Lord. "I will counsel you."[4]

Continues Lee Downing,

"Just how God's plan for a particular life will be revealed, no one can say. He does not deal alike with His children, but each may be led on to prayer experiences (almost) too rich to be described."[5]

Ray: *I was walking alone at Glen Eyrie, the Colorado Springs Navigators' Conference Grounds, asking the Lord for some insight into the future. What I'm about to tell you I've only shared before with my wife and then recently with a few close brothers, because it's actually embarrassingly wonderful.*

I don't remember exactly how, but God gave me Acts 1:8:

"Ye shall receive power, after that the Holy Ghost is come upon you: and ye shall [witness of Me] . . . unto the uttermost part of the earth" (KJV).

It was actually breathtaking to think that God might use me around the world. I didn't even tell Anne for quite some time. But when I did, she mounted a world map on hardboard, and from that time we've put stickers on every place where the Lord has let me preach of Him. That map is now peppered with red dots, witnessing to God's faithfulness to keep His promise to me. Besides that, He allows me to preach by radio to vast areas of the world every Sunday over Far East Broadcasting Company. And I don't think His promises to me are finished yet!

Now, believe this: God's plan is for you to believe that God has a great plan for you! The only question is: Are you willing to believe Him and get in on it?

David believed God, and what a life! He wrote, "Though I am surrounded by troubles, you will bring me safely through them. . . . The Lord will work out his plans for my life—for your lovingkindness, Lord, continues forever."[6]

The two of us want to say to you loud and clear that if you are a child of God's, His blueprint for you is more exciting and fulfilling than you dream. You're just one little human life, but God will catch you up into eternity. His plans for you are so vast and important. Whatever your age, now is the time to believe that God has a great future for you and to cooperate with Him by getting stars in your eyes, in looking up, in letting His plans become yours.

"I know the plans I have for you, says the Lord, plans for welfare and not for evil, to give you a future and a hope."[7]

Ray: *I remember the first time that verse ever struck me.*

Anne: *It was several years ago, when we wanted so badly to accept an invitation to minister for a few months in Afghanistan, and we couldn't see the way clear. We had to make sure our dear church was in the best possible hands in our absence, if God was going to pull it off.*

Ray: *Then I was reading through Jeremiah, and those words just climbed right off the page to me: "I know the plans I have for you, says the Lord, plans for welfare and not for evil, to give you a future and a hope."*

And we went to Afghanistan for three months, and it was a fabulous time of growth in our lives and good for the church, too.

We've repeated this little poem to each other many times through the years:

> He knows, He loves, He cares;
> Nothing this truth can dim.
> He gives the very best to those
> Who leave the choice with Him.[8]

It's interesting that, whether a person is over-motivated and needing control or under-motivated and needing a spur, the answer is always discovering, believing and obeying the Lord's plans for his life.

Don't be satisfied with watching others live! In our "day of the spectator" we've become those who live secondhand. We watch people supposedly live on television. We watch players in a game. We live vicariously.

God calls on you to live fully, now—not to be in the bleachers, but on the field, not spectators but participants.

Go after the things of God. Discover what His specific plans are for you, and for the Future You.

Ray: *I can't forget the experience of visiting my good friend Rolf in his last days of cancer, just before he died. He was suffering. I asked him, "Rolf, do you wish God would take you home to heaven?"*

We knew each other very well.

He said, "Oh, no! Tomorrow may be my finest hour, the very day for which I was made!"

The future belongs to God. My friend, are you listening? Joshua says, "Consecrate yourself, for tomorrow the Lord will do wonders among you."[9]

Put this book down right now, long enough to pray, "Lord, use these remaining chapters in my thinking— and in my life! I need freshening. I need new power over old temptations. I need to turn a new corner. I want to stride into the coming 'future-shock world' with all confidence in you. I want to finish my course with joy.

"Lay it on me, Father. Tell it to me straight. I'm humble. I'm listening."

Friend, God has a wonderful plan for your life, and only you can make that plan fail.

Footnotes

1. Lee H. Downing, *God's Plan for My Life* (Pearl River, New York: Africa Inland Mission).
2. Colossians 1:9, *NASB.*
3. Proverbs 8:14, *NASB.*
4. Psalm 32:8, *NASB.*
5. Downing, *God's Plan for My Life.*
6. Psalm 138:7,8, *TLB.*
7. Jeremiah 29:11, *RSV.*
8. Unknown.
9. Joshua 3:5, *NASB.*

2.

To Win You Must Begin

Life is shaped like a funnel. But everything depends on which way you go into it.

The worldling goes in at the big end, where everything looks grandiose and inviting and limitless in possibilities and freedom. Then life for him narrows down into boring smallness.

The Christian goes in the other end; "narrow is the gate" that leads to his life. But then he finds that it broadens out into beautiful freedom, into glorious newness. It keeps opening and opening and opening into God's vast will and righteousness and pleasures. There is no boredom! There is no smallness when you walk with God.

Within that life with Him there is continual newness and expansion. You can begin again and again and again! When you take a look at the life you've been leading, you may be thinking, "What's the use? I'm in a rut. I'm on the way to a dead end. I'll settle for what I am and that's all I'm going to be." Friend, low expectation spells death.

We want to tell you that the Christian life—*lived really Christian*—offers you wide horizons. It offers you great new beginnings. It's possible to have a fresh start. Whoever you are, you can begin again.

The Christian should *normally* experience constant renewal. Ephesians 4:23 says to "be renewed in the spirit of your minds" (*RSV*). And that's in the present tense. "Keep on being renewed," in the spiritual youthfulness that God wants to give you. It begins in the mind, in the thinking center. God wants to change the entire way you look at your life.

For instance, for the two of us—and our church,—about eight years ago, God opened up the vision of living by three priorities: God first, the Body of Christ second, and our work and witness in the world third.[1] There's nothing new about that in Scripture; the implications of it are all the way through the New Testament. Where had our eyes been? But the concept of it was so new to us—longtime Christians in our early forties—that it has changed our lives and kept changing our lives ever since, as well as the lives of thousands of others.

We had no idea what was about to happen; we only knew we were hungry for more of God. We had no idea that that marvelous funnel-shaped life God had given us was about to expand immeasurably! It's true, you know, that in the Christian life you will stumble upon wonder after wonder—and every wonder will be true.

Anne: *My friend Joan had been a Christian for three years when she began to be weary of conformity to her particular world and to long for more of Christ. She's a chic, sleek young matron with husband, family and home all in the class of those who have "arrived." Money, beauty, no problems! But the Holy Spirit was tugging at her.*

She came to see us one summer day and talked over

16

her projected fall plans: volunteer jobs, committees, daily tennis. We didn't influence her one way or another, but we promised we'd pray. By fall she'd cut loose from everything, and she was free all day long every day to be a child of God, a wife, a mother, a member of the Body of Christ!

It began a whole new life. George and Joan together are taking new steps for Christ every day, reshaping their finances, their business, their life-style to glorify God. They've never been more happily married, and they've never been a more powerful influence on the secular world where God has put them.

Paul says, "I will be one who lives in the fresh newness of life"![2] And, "If anyone is in Christ, he is a new creation; the old has passed away, behold, the new has come."[3] That last phrase really means that the "new has come *and is coming*"—a continual process. The normal life of the growing man and woman of God is that the new keeps coming.

And listen to this: If He can renew individuals, He can also renew the whole world! The whole plan of history from God's point of view ends in glorious newness—in a new heaven and a new earth. If our little personal world is under constant renewal, His grand conclusion will be a mind-blower. "Behold," says God in the book of Revelation, "I make *all things new*" (21:5, *KJV*, italics added).

And that is God's way; that is God's great principle.

You see, the things of man get older and get less. But the things of God get renewed and get more! And that is what God does for any person who trusts Him. We are "being transformed into likeness to Him, from one degree of splendor to another."[4] You have not yet begun to see all that God wants to do for you.

17

We know what it's like to feel dull. Separately, or together, the two of us many times have cried out to the Lord, and He has come through! Time after time we've experienced the gift of God's beginning again in our lives. He has given us either a crisis of refreshing, or a process of refreshing.

Ray: *Sometimes it's crisis. I'll just share my heart with you: Sometimes I've been devastated by weakness and sin. I've been unable to manage myself or my thoughts; my head was not on right at all. I remember once I got down on the floor and wept before God, stretched out flat. I thought, "Ortlund, you're through. You're no good, period. You'll never be anything." But wonderfully, the Spirit of God began to encourage me again.*

Or sometimes God has used a sharp word from a friend that bluntly and correctly confirmed my worst fears about myself! But this friend would then make suggestions to give me hope. And I would begin to receive God's grace, and God would give me another fresh start.

Maybe you need this new start. Only God can untangle your mess, but He can do it. You can't—but God can. You feel fixed, immobile, frozen where you are; God can free you! Maybe you've had a wrong entanglement with somebody. Can God make it right? Yes, He can!

Maybe your marriage has gotten stale. God can give you a new marriage—to the same person. Maybe you have a deeply ingrained habit of gossip. Don't swallow the school of thinking that you're the product of your past, and there's no way out. *God is the God of new beginnings.*

The following might sound like a hearts-and-flowers

story, told to the tune of a violin, but we tell it to encourage both you and us that the sky's the limit.

Some young people in a former church of ours went visiting Sunday afternoons at a "county poor farm." They introduced Aunt Nancy to Jesus Christ—Aunt Nancy, who was 98 years old, bedridden, and who was so destitute she didn't even own the nightgown she was wearing.

Aunt Nancy's new spiritual dreams had no limits. She wanted to give something to help support missionaries! Somebody had given her an African violet plant, and she asked a nurse for a second pot and divided it. Pretty soon her bed was surrounded with violets. She was selling them to anyone who passed; the word spread. People thought it was "cute" and came to buy or just to contribute; and when Aunt Nancy was just past a hundred, as a two-year-old Christian, she was partially supporting a missionary nurse in India.

We two have experienced newness in our lives time and time again, and we expect to in the future as well. God says, "I will heal their backsliding, I will love them freely."[5] That's our God.

Anne: *All my life I have wrestled with my tongue. Well, actually, many times I didn't wrestle too hard. I have a sense of the dramatic, and I can always make a good story better. If the truth is "three," "four" will often slip out of my mouth. If the truth is "forty," I may say "fifty." The world calls this exaggerating, but I had to get desperate enough, several years ago, to see that God calls it lying.*

So at the next opportunity, which happened to be a New Year's Eve service when our church congregation was having a time of "waiting on God," I, the pastor's wife, stood up before them all and told them what I'd picked to be my verse for the new year, 1 Peter 3:10: If you want a happy, good life, keep control of your tongue, and guard your lips from telling lies" (TLB). I explained to them my problem and asked them to pray for me. Boy, it was hard!

I had a sense of immediate improvement. When I was talking I'd be conscious of a need for caution, and I began to get downright exhilarated over my new victory. I have no idea how many of those dear people actually were in prayer over my request, but that fall, perhaps nine months later, a beautiful young housewife, half my age, asked me very gently how I was doing with my tongue, and she said she'd been praying for me all year. I really hugged her. That kind of loving concern and prayer for me had broken the back of a lifelong habit.

Onesimus was a fugitive in exile, afraid to go back to his home and his job. Then Paul interceded to Onesimus' superior, and he was welcomed back and got a chance to begin again—and not as a slave but as a brother.[6]

John Mark became a quitter, and ran away from Paul and his ministry. But later on Paul wrote in a letter, "Bring me Mark, for he is important to me."[7] So we know that for Mark, too, God became the God of new beginnings.

God sometimes identifies Himself as "the God of Jacob." Do you know what "Jacob" means? Supplanter, grasper, greedy person! God says, "I'm the God of the greedy person." Isn't that amazing? Unpromising Jacob! But God saw behind his meanness an opportunity for His grace.

God appeared five times in the life of Jacob; five times He met with him in special ways.

One time He said to him, "What is your name?"

He said, "My name is Jacob" (supplanter, greedy person, cheat).

And God said, "You shall no longer be called that, but you shall be called Israel—Prince with God!" (the name still given to all his descendants, and their land as well).

The promises for renewal are all there. But for you, what's the price? The price is two-fold: one is repentance, and the other is faith. That's what we have all through the Scriptures, a "running commentary," a call for repentance and for faith. Let God make some changes in your life. Acknowledge your need for the changes—that's repentance—and turn around. Get going by His grace and strength in a new direction.

You see in Ephesians 4:22 that you are to "put off your old nature which belongs to your former manner of life and is corrupt through deceitful lusts" (*RSV*). Christianity has its negative side. There are some things you've got to quit doing. In verse 17 He says, "You must no longer live as the Gentiles [unbelieving world] do" (*RSV*).

Anne: *Two of my favorite words are "eliminate" and "concentrate." There is no way God can fill us with the positive if we're not willing to give up the negative. You can't have a garden by just tending the flowers; you've got to pull the weeds, too. It's the combination. God told Jeremiah that he needed to "pluck up and to break down, to destroy and overthrow," and he needed "to build and to plant."*[8]

Maybe you wonder why you're dry, why you're not spiritually alert. Peter, in Acts 3:19, pled with his hearers, "Repent therefore, and turn again, that your sins may be blotted out, that *times of refreshing may come* from the presence of the Lord" (*RSV*, italics added).

God wants to give you refreshing! But in order to begin anew, your part is to repent, to be truly sorry that you got caught up in all that.

Don't be like some people who "spend their whole lives perfecting their faults." God's Word says that a time comes when it will be too late—when those who are filthy will remain filthy still, when those who are vile will remain vile.

And, friend, by the time you're 35 or beyond, you've gotten into a lot of cement, into fixed mind-sets! So repentance before it's too late may be a wrenching, jolting experience. But do it, do it!

Ray: *If you will repent and believe God—He puts it this way in Joel: "I will restore to you the years which the swarming locust has eaten."* Listen, God will do that for you. We've seen people with hard expressions come out of tough, defeated, discouraged lives—who begin again with God, and they actually have brighter, happier, faces. It happens!*

But repent and believe—do both, not just repent. Until you believe God, repentance is just a "trip," and it's no fun. You need to believe what God can do for you.

There's a true story of a couple who failed on their farm in the depression days. So they took the assets they had and bought a little drugstore in a Midwest community. Crops were terrible; people had no money to buy things; and the drugstore was doing poorly.

One day the wife, Dorothy Hustead, sat at the window watching people drive by—people traveling across the country over that Midwest highway in their hot, dirty cars. She said to her husband Ted, "Do you know what these people need? They need a drink of water." She said, "Let's give them what every drugstore has, but

22

let's advertise it! Then they'll stop into ours."

And so for 25 miles in every direction they built signs along the roads:

FREE ICE WATER
WALL DRUGSTORE
WALL, SOUTH DAKOTA

And it tickled people's sense of humor, and they began to come in to get free ice water—and to buy.

It sounds like such a little thing, but it was a great idea. Those signs now appear all over the world. Do you know what you can read on the thirty-eighth parallel in Korea?

FREE ICE WATER
WALL DRUGSTORE
5,280 MILES

In Paris: "5,961 MILES TO WALL DRUGSTORE: FREE ICE WATER." Underground subway in London: "5,160 MILES ... FREE ICE WATER."

God has given you plenty of promises. Now, for a new beginning in your life, you must get a plan. That's what this book is all about.

You may be thinking, "You don't know my particular obstacle. My case is special." Then, for you, God will give a special wisdom for your particular "end run" around that obstacle. God always creates those very situations in each life which will show His power best!

So ask Him for creative wisdom. Proverbs 30:24–28 tells us how God gives special, hidden wisdom to each of His creatures to overcome what they must overcome:

1. Ants are weak. But they compensate by anticipating future times when weakness would be a drawback—and they turn out to be winners.

2. Cliff badgers are delicate and small. So they compensate by staying in an environment where they're protected—and there they do very well.

3. Locusts don't have any leader. So they compensate by fitting in, cooperating, going *with*, not alone—and they survive just fine.

4. Lizards are easy to catch and kill, and yet they simply disregard danger and live boldly; they're found in the number-one places of the earth. And 3,000 years after these words were written, they're far from an extinct species.

Why did God bother to put space in His holy Word to tell us about these little creatures of His? He says they all have drawbacks seemingly too great for them to find success—*but He gives them special wisdom to make it.* The point is, don't make excuses. Don't procrastinate. Just seek out from God His special ways for you to carry out His wonderful plans for your life.

Ray: *Repent from your present undirected life; believe that God can start you off fresh—then what? Well, you need very specific, measurable goals.*

You need life goals, down in black and white, for you to pray over and be guided by. If your only life goal is to "be a good Christian," how will you know at the end of life whether you made it or not? That's too vague.

And you need short-term goals. We've been setting short-term goals for years. ("Between now and October I spend five minutes each day rejoicing in God...." "By April 15 lose five pounds...." "Fast every noon hour until our child is submissive to the Lord....")

And we hold each other accountable.

Goal-setting is nothing new. F. B. Meyer made seven rules for himself to live by every day:

1. Make a daily, definite, audible consecration of yourself to God. Say it out loud: "Lord, today I give myself anew to You."

2. Tell God that you are *willing to be made willing,* to do all that He wants you to do.

3. Reckon on Christ to do His part perfectly in your life.

4. Confess sin instantly.

5. Submit to Christ every temptation and every care.

6. Keep in touch with Christ. (Read the Word and good books; seek places and people where Jesus really is.)

7. Expect the Holy Ghost to work in, with, and for you.[10]

In these years of your life, as you contemplate living the second half, what will God reveal to you? Will He give you new "points of departure"? Is it too late?

Ray: *The man who was to become the apostle Paul was a strong, middle-aged man, a member of the top-dog Sanhedrin, upper-crust, trained, strong-willed, and sure of himself. Let's call him "set in his ways."*

Last week I got new hope again for my own "second half of life" as I was studying to preach about Paul and read this:

"[At the time of Paul's conversion] He was already near middle age,* with the vast task of the world's evangelization ahead of him. God seemed in no hurry: . . . His conversion was by far the most vital influence in Paul's life. Ancestry, Pharisaic training, Hellenistic education were fused by it into the character which the Holy Spirit formed and fashioned over the fourteen years of training (as a new Christian). At length, in God's good time, the door opened, and the events of half a lifetime assumed final and complete significance."[11]

Maybe the reading of this book is the confrontation you need on your personal Damascus Road. There's no time like now.

Someone said, "To win, you must begin."

Footnotes

1. Raymond C. Ortlund, *Lord, Make My Life a Miracle* (Glendale: G/L Publications, 1974).
2. Philippians 3:11, *TLB*.
3. 2 Corinthians 5:17, *RSV*.
4. 2 Corinthians 3:18, Charles B. Williams, *The New Testament in the Language of the People* (Chicago: Moody Press, 1960).
5. Hosea 14:4, *KJV*.
6. See Philemon.
7. See 2 Timothy 4:11.
8. Jeremiah 1:10, *RSV*.
9. Joel 2:25, *RSV*.
10. Bernice Carlson Flynn, "Their Goal Was Mastery of Self," *Christian Life*, Vol. 21, No. 9, p. 12.
11. E. M. Blaiklock, *Tyndale New Testament Commentaries, The Acts of the Apostles* (Grand Rapids: Eerdmans Publishing Co., 1959), p. 90. (*Acts 7:58 speaks of Paul as a "young man," but J. Rawson Lumby in *The Cambridge Bible, The Acts of the Apostles* [New York: Cambridge University Press, p. 95] says, "The Greek word applied to persons up to the age of 40.... Paul may well have been between 30 and 40 years of age.") Used by permission.

3.

Look Out! Enemies Are Coming!

Recently we were cheering each other up with that old Clairol commercial, "You're not getting older, you're getting better."

"Yeah," piped up our 10-year-old Nels. "One of you's getting older, and the other's getting better."

We didn't dare ask which was which.

There's something insidious about this aging business —a smog that drifts in from the thinking of the world— and it needs to be dealt with head-on.

There's a story about a little girl who climbed up on the lap of Dr. Dewitt Talmage and looked at his white hair and wrinkles and then asked, "Did God make you?"

"Yes," he said.

Then she asked, "Did God make me, too?"

Dr. Talmage said, "Yes."

"Well," said the little girl, "Don't you think He's doing a better job now than He used to?"

Stories like that are cute, but depressing. You really begin to think you're not only getting older, you're getting worse. And it is the actual truth that for people who don't know the Lord and walk with Him, it's downhill all the way.

For instance, here's what Plato said happens to the

mind: "Experience takes away more than it adds. Young people are nearer ideas than old men." Thanks a lot, Plato!

What happens to the body? Well, you've got plenty of cartoons like the matron in the beauty parlor who remarks, "This aging gracefully is a heck of a lot of work!"

What happens to the spirit? That French sage Ernest Dimnet writes, "Young saints are not scarce; an old one is a delightful exception."

Dimnet goes on to say that the typical modern lifestyle "drives [people] to organized nothingness.... Their endless complaint is that they never have any time, and are glad occasionally to be sick, in order to steal a little rest. Yet they dread solitude, and their one antonym for amusement is boredom.... Time for thought they have not.... They live in their most elementary instincts, seeking happiness in pleasure, affairs, or power.... Altogether, life does just the opposite of what it is supposed to do; it travels away from thought."[1]

Anne: *I remember my university president's address to the student body when I was a freshman—his opening address for fall semester. He told us that five years after we graduated, most of us would be uneducated again.*

Well, we know what you're thinking. Something rises up inside of you, as it does us, and you say, "But I refuse to be like the dull, grey masses! For me there's going to be a better way." Right?

And there is, there is! There's a way to victory. There's a way to make life better and better, always upward right to the end. There's a way to watch God's light shine brighter and brighter in your life just as Proverbs 4:18 says, "But the path of the righteous is like the light of dawn, which shines brighter and brighter until

28

full day" (*RSV*). There's a way for you to be a winner!

What you need is God's set of weapons for striking down every one of those enemies of the second half of life, those elements of the aging process which would defeat you along the way. One by one, God can help you cut them down. Others may succumb. Well, *they* may turn into bitter, self-centered old codgers and biddies, but you're not going to. Not when all God's weapons are available to you. Grab hold of them, and start the battle!

ENEMY ONE: COMPLAINING. This is the sin that so grieved the Lord that He decreed that no complaining Israelites traveling in the wilderness could enter the Promised Land.

And who were the complainers? God said, "Except for Joshua and Caleb, don't let anybody over 20 years old go in!"² Apparently, complaining naturally begins at about twenty.

WEAPON: Adapt the attitude of the aged Paul in Philippians 4:12: "I have learned the secret of contentment in every situation" (*TLB*). Friend, think deeply about that. Make a list of your "situations." Before God, are you *contented* in every one? "Pray in" the spirit of contentment into every area of your life. What a difference it will make in the facial expression of that Future You!

Ray: *A few years ago at Lake Avenue Church, I was convinced that we needed to start a second morning service. I presented the need and plan to the congregation, and, to my amazement, they voted not to do it. I was disappointed, of course, but I told the Lord that I really believe He speaks through His local Body of believers, and so I should be contented with the present situation and go on.*

I really believe that when I didn't have a "fit" over the decision, the Lord used that to change attitudes, and three months later we began two morning services at the request of the congregation.

ENEMY TWO: PRIDE. The new subconscious mood growing within you through the years, "I'm okay, you're so-so."

Uzziah was a fabulous king of Judah until he was established and had made it. Then he turned subtly proud (see 2 Chron. 26:16), and in the second half of his life he was a useless leper. God was through with him.

WEAPON: 1 PETER 5:6: "If you will humble yourselves under the mighty hand of God, *in his good time* he will lift you up" (*TLB*, italics added). In the second half! Humble and exalted, both, all the way through life!

ENEMY THREE: RIGIDITY, DOGMATISM. In the middle years we start getting into ruts, and we're unwilling to climb out. This is no doubt why God told the Israelites in public service that they had to retire at the age of 50.[3] After that they were too unteachable.

Anne: *This is one of the enemies I fear most. I think I must have been born with a mind that jumps too soon to conclusions.*

I can't help that tendency to leap; my mind has hind legs like a frog. But the Lord—and Ray—have been helping me to back off again, take second looks at situations, and not become dogmatic over issues that aren't settled.

That is, I think I'm less dogmatic!

WEAPON: Again, the words of Paul in his latter days: "I don't mean to say I am perfect. I haven't learned all I should even yet, but I keep working toward that day."[4]

Hannah Whitall Smith at age 70 wrote,

"We must be perfectly content to have our advice

rejected by the younger (adults), and our experience ignored. Were we willing for this, I am convinced the young would much more often be glad to profit by what is called the 'wisdom of the old'; but as it is, they are afraid to ask advice because they know they will be expected to follow it, whether it commends itself to them or not, and because they fear the old will feel hurt if they do not.

"Perfect freedom in asking advice can only exist along with perfect freedom not to follow that advice."[5]

ENEMY FOUR: AN INFERIORITY COMPLEX. The impulse to say "I can't."

God told Moses to go say to Pharaoh, "Let My people go." Moses said, "O Lord, I'm not a good speaker."

"Who makes mouths?" Jehovah asked him. "Isn't it I, the Lord? Who makes a man so that he can speak or not speak, see or not see, hear or not hear? Now go ahead and do as I tell you, for I will help you to speak well, and I will tell you what to say."[6]

WEAPON: FAITH. The doer is not you but God!

Bob Turner was 30. He had a Christian wife who invited us to their home one time for dinner. "Don't talk church to me," said Bob. "I don't want to go because I'm afraid of people. I don't have any friends except my wife, and I don't want any."

His parting shot was, "If I ever do come to church, I'll be in the back row, and don't talk to me."

Eventually he did start coming, and we kept our word and let him bolt out the door afterward, unspoken to.

But finally Bob met Jesus Christ. He was fabulously saved, not only from his sins but from his hung-up self. Six months later he was the church's number-one greeter and hand-pumper. He was in charge of all games and icebreakers for the church couples' club. And he was singing bass in the men's quartet.

An inferiority complex is nothing but an insult to God and His power. "I can't" says that your thinking is centered on yourself and your circumstances, instead of on Him. So, you're defeated before you start.

So was Peter when he was out in that water, and ready to sink. All he had to do was get his eyes back on that wonderful Source of all help. His words were short—they had to be! "Lord, save me!"[7]

That changed everything.

Anne: *There have been times when my dear husband has come home from church overwhelmed with the enormity of his job. Several times in the course of our 16-year ministry here at Lake Avenue Congregational Church, Ray has come home declaring, "I can't do it. The job's too big for me."*

Bless his heart, at those moments I've played the role of the tough guy. "Yes, that's true, you can't. Whatever made you think you could? Either the Lord will have to do it through you, or it won't be done at all."

I don't know what goes on between God and him when he's gone out into the night from conversations like these, to hassle it all out. I only know that I've witnessed an attitude of rest come in the midst of work, and of peace in the midst of stress. "This is the Lord's doing; it is marvelous in our eyes."[8]

ENEMY FIVE: MATERIALISM, ANXIETY TO KEEP WHAT YOU HAVE. W. R. Simmons researchers have discovered that Cadillac owners are more anxious people than Volkswagen owners. Does that mean that owning a Cadillac brings a person anxiety and a lot more worries? Not at all, researcher David S. Viscott says. "It's just that Cadillac owners are usually older, and older people are nearly *always* more 'anxious'.... They are living longer, but enjoying it less. . . . A Cadillac mates nicely with cashmere coats, a home in the 'best' part of town. . . . These people have a whole Sears catalog of anxieties and hang-ups."[9]

WEAPON: GENEROSITY. Let go! Every time you sense you have more than your brother, give to him. That's so simple, it's almost unknown. It's so obvious, it's universally overlooked and untried. Have you taken a good look lately at the struggling students around you, and the retired friends on pension? Love ought to flow through the Body of Christ through money, as well as other ways. And respond to a plea for help from overseas. Let your heart stay tender and generous.

A little boy had his hand caught in a cookie jar, and couldn't get it out. Then his mother discovered why: he was holding a cookie! If he'd been willing to open his hand, he could have been released. And he wanted freedom—but not at the price of letting go of that cookie.

Read 2 Corinthians 8:12–15 (in fact, all of chapters 8 and 9), and discover that when you're willing to let go, God will make sure you never lack. But you'll be freed from the awful tyranny of being possessed by possessions.

ENEMY SIX: THE TEMPTATION TO LET DOWN THE STANDARDS. To seek easier ways. Maybe the last child has gone off to college; you could sleep in on a Sunday morning, and who would know? Or the money is finally available for a weekend cabin or boat. . . .

WEAPON: HEBREWS 3:14: "If we are faithful to the end, trusting God just as we did when we first became Christians, we will share in all that belongs to Christ" (*TLB*).

Trusting God *in the same way* you did as a new Christian! Do you remember? Jesus says in Revelation 2:5, "Think about those times of your first love (how different now!) and turn back to me again" (*TLB*).

This isn't to say that you might not get that cabin or boat; but, friend, there are so many enemies to putting God first! Slash down that enemy of spiritual degeneration and live in the glowing newness of your first love, all the rest of your life.

We know a wonderful example of this kind of person. Cecil is a business man in his late fifties who loves boats. When he bought his very first one, he named it the *Seek Ye*, and he hung a framed verse in the cabin which read, "Seek ye first the kingdom of God, and his righteousness; and all these things shall be added unto you."[10] "Lord," said Cecil, "I dedicate to you my Friday-night-and-Saturday boat."

That was many years ago, and these days Cecil is still boating—no longer in *Seek Ye I* but *Seek Ye V*. Meantime he's taught Sunday School classes through the years, been a church trustee, chaired building committees, and done many other great things for God. Best of all, as was said of Wesley, Cecil is "out of breath pursuing souls": an indefatigable and effective fisher of men, who lives in the fresh newness of his first love.

ENEMY SEVEN: THE DESIRE TO APPEAR INSTEAD OF TO BE. This one is dangerous and subtle. Sports cars and toupees may be just fine—but they can devastate you if they're a substitute for *becoming*.

If you're facing the second half of life and you sense you're not becoming, panic may drive you *backward in appearance*. But remember: careful grooming may make you look 20 years younger, but it won't fool a flight of stairs!

"There is no one," says columnist-philosopher Max Lerner, "who turns me off quite so badly as the middle-aged professor-turned-hippie or parent-turned-hippie, who apes the ways of the young."[11]

"It used to be," said playwright Arthur Miller, "that the adolescent couldn't wait to grow up; now the grown-ups try to act and sound like adolescents. What happened is that both collided in the middle going the opposite directions."[12]

Again, if you're in the second half of life and you sense you're not becoming, panic may drive you to *look more affluent.* The urge to keep up with the Joneses—also your age—may propel you to building a bigger house like theirs, buying a bigger car like theirs—and acquiring a much bigger debt.

Putting on a false exterior to appear like your brother is a very old trick. Jacob did it. All it took for him was Esau's clothes and some furry skins, and he thought he'd made it. But all the rest of his life people played tricks on the trickster.

One ruse always leads to another. The outside must continually be shored up, because the inside is falling apart. All this pathetic seeking to *appear* is the opposite of 2 Corinthians 4:16: "So we do not lose heart. Though our outer nature is wasting away, our inner nature is being renewed every day" (*RSV*).

WEAPON: SURRENDER TO GOD. So simple! Like any flower that lifts its head and says, "Paint me like you want me."

Anne: *Or—well, almost. Ray says some day he's going to take me to a desert island for six months and find out what color my hair really is.*

ENEMY EIGHT: DULLNESS, PESSIMISM. Are you no longer expecting miracles? Has it been a long time since God seemed very near, since your heart leaped with joy over some new truth, since you sang songs at midnight —did the offbeat thing—out of sheer exuberance? If it

35

has, probably sins have clogged the pipes—sins of omission and commission.

Anne: *Recently I heard a physician already at retirement age but in good health, wonder aloud if he should take a year off to get some additional training. Fantastic! I hope he does.*

One of my life goals is to serve the Lord together with Ray (God willing) until we're at least 85, seeing Acts 1:8 fulfilled abundantly all the way. I feel in my bones that because Ray even dared to title his first book Lord, Make My Life a Miracle, *God will continue publicly confirming that his life is just that.*

Not everybody can write a book, but any Christian can pray that prayer; and then stand back—look out!—for all that God will do for him.

WEAPON: ACTS 3:19: "Now change your mind and attitude to God [repent!] and turn to him so he can cleanse away your sins and send you wonderful times of refreshment from the presence of the Lord" (*TLB*).

It's always time for a new start. Read Acts 4:22 and shout whoopee!—"For the man was more than forty years old on whom this miracle was done" (*NASB*).

ENEMY NINE: LOOKING BACKWARD IN REGRET. The very posture of looking backward is unscriptural and disobedient. Don't ever blubber about the "good old days." God's principle is always that the best wine is last; that the new covenant is better than the old; that heaven follows earth. Live all your life on tiptoe to enjoy each fresh new thing God is just bringing about. "Forgetting the past and looking forward to what lies ahead, I strain to reach the end of the race."[13] *Phil 3:13-14*

And it's even more devastating to look back at the errors made, the sins committed.

Anne: *There are plenty of bad memories in my past that I could drag up if I worked on it. But God loves to release me from everything that would haunt me and hold me down. He's on my side! I love those beautiful words in Hebrews, "See to it that no one comes short of the grace of God."[14] He doesn't want me to miss any of His grace, His mercy and forgiveness!*

So it's up to me to take my past failures and say, "Lord Jesus Christ, thank you that the blood you shed on the cross was shed for all my past. And the Bible tells me that on the basis of the cross, you'll remember my sins no more. You cast them behind your back. As far as the east is from the west, you've removed my transgressions from me. I walk away totally free!"

Many Christians have their sins cancelled as far as God is concerned, but the power of their memory is still holding them down. *He* is the One who breaks the power of cancelled sin; *He* is the One who sets the prisoner free.

WEAPON: JOYOUS ANTICIPATION OF THE FUTURE. In Christ, you're free to dream, to have large visions of what God will do through you. Listen, God wants you to know that He has dealt thoroughly with your sin, so that you are truly a new person in Christ Jesus; that you can do all things through Christ who strengthens you; that Jesus has really "paid it all"; and that He means to make you into something wonderful, to the glory of His name.

Ray: *Anne and I love a couple of brothers-in-law we know, one now in heaven and one remaining, who always had their faces set toward the future. Herbert Nicholson and Paul Waterhouse were two missionaries who, separately in several different countries, went hard after God through their long careers here and there around the world. They didn't escape the discouragements that every soldier of the cross faces. But they had a saying with which they greeted each other and ended every conversation every time their paths crossed. "Kori-kawa," they'd shout to each other. "From now on!"*

Anne: *Often when Ray and I get up licking our wounds from one thing or another, one of us will say, "Kori-kawa!" It's so great to know noble-minded people whose lives rub off on you a little.*
A big part of being noble is the ability to think future.

ENEMY TEN: FEAR OF THE NEW, OVERCAUTIOUSNESS. Instead of living on the defensive, take the offensive. Somebody wrote, "In youth we want to change the world. In old age we want to change the youth."

Do you sense yourself too often reacting instead of acting?

In the fourteenth and fifteenth chapters of 2 Chronicles we have the story of 35 years of glory for Asa, king of Judah. But then in chapter 16, in the thirty-sixth year of his reign—can you imagine?—King Asa fell apart. Some puny little enemy came marching toward him, and for the first time he began to wring his hands, worry and make gestures of compromise.

For the first time Asa crossed over from the offensive position to the defensive; he succumbed to that monster —defensiveness—who rises up to try to weaken the second half of anybody's life. Asa became just another victim—the typically fearful, overcautious, over-conservative old fuddy-duddy which God never intended anybody to be. So in his last years, Asa fizzled out.

WEAPON: LIVING IN GOD'S PRESENCE! Ephesians 6 says to stay forever *in Christ*, to stand against the enemy in that position. John 15 says to abide there and don't leave. Surrounded by Him, living consciously in Him, is like living your life protected all around by an invisible shield. Plenty of people won't understand why you're so full of courage and optimism!

His very presence is all the protection you need—not just the theoretical knowledge of it, but oh, friend, the mental discipline of practicing His presence moment by moment! He will keep you secure.

That armor was even available to King Asa. He knew very well the Ninety-first Psalm: "We live within the shadow of the Almighty. . . . He alone is my refuge, my place of safety. . . . His faithful promises are your armor. Now you don't need to be afraid."[15]

So these are the enemies of the second half of life.

Hosea 7:9 is a pathetic verse about Israel: "Worshiping foreign gods has sapped their strength, but they don't know it. Ephraim's hair is turning gray, and he doesn't even realize how weak and old he is" (*TLB*).

Do you notice what speeded up the aging process? *Worshiping foreign gods.* Verse 8 says, "My people *mingle with the heathen*" (italics added).

Listen, there's nothing that can age you like taking on the spirit of the world and mingling among the worriers, the jet set, the status seekers, the materialists, the fearful, the rat-racers, the competitors. There's nothing like these contacts to achieve that sagging posture and those old, bored eyes. Cousin What's-his-name will see you after a few months and he'll think, "My, how he's aged."

Combat age with godliness! Live in God. Stay young all your life by being totally equipped with all His weapons:

1. Contentment
2. Humility

3. Teachableness
4. Faith
5. Generosity
6. First love
7. Surrender to God
8. Continual freshness of spirit
9. Joyous anticipation of the future
10. Living in God's presence

The godly woman of Proverbs 31 has her priorities straight. Verse 30 says, "Charm can be deceptive and beauty doesn't last, but a woman who fears and reverences God shall be greatly praised" (*TLB*). That's why, says verse 25, she "has no fear of old age"!

A man who is "having a ball" living the second half of his life is Dr. Karl Menninger, the world-famous psychiatrist. In his eighty-first year, *Time* magazine said of him, he "still throws off sparks aplenty."

As we face seriously these enemies of the second half of life, listen to these words of Dr. Menninger in his book, *Whatever Became of Sin?*: "Doesn't anyone sin any more? Or doesn't anyone believe in sin? Or is nothing now a sin?"[16]

Friend, over your head at this moment is at least one of these ten enemy giants (maybe many) poised to strike. If you think of him impersonally, he will eventually overcome you. But if you address him as "my own sin," he will look at you in blank astonishment and then wither and fall backward to the ground.

Look at these enemies. They're not ghosties and ghoulies and long-leggeddy beasties from some external source; they're sins—probably *your* sins:

1. Complaining
2. Pride
3. Rigidity, dogmatism
4. An inferiority complex

5. Materialism
6. Relaxing the standards
7. The desire to appear instead of to be
8. Dullness, pessimism
9. Looking backward
10. Fear of the new, overcautiousness.

Put your finger on them, one by one. Own them as your own personal sins, the enemies of your soul, the destroyer of the Future You. Ask God to forgive you specifically. Ask Him to cleanse you, refresh you, give you a new start. Ask Him for honest victory over each of these.

Now think of Romans 12:1,2 in a new light. So you're facing the second half of your life and you're a little scared?

Verse 1 says, "I plead with you to give your [body] to God" (*TLB*).

Your body, a living sacrifice. Let Him be in charge of whatever happens to it in the future.

Verse 2 says that then, only then, will you be a "new and different person with a fresh newness in all you do and think. Then you will learn from your own experience his ways will really satisfy you."

Three cheers!

Footnotes

1. Ernest Dimnet, *The Art of Thinking* (New York: Fawcett World, 1971), pp. 79, 80.
2. See Numbers 14:26–36.
3. See Numbers 8:23–26.
4. Philippians 3:12, *TLB*.
5. Hannah Whitall Smith, "The Threshold Years," *Moody Monthly*.
6. Exodus 4:11,12, *TLB*.
7. See Matthew 14.
8. Psalm 118:23, *RSV*.
9. David S. Viscott, *Los Angeles Times*.

10. Matthew 6:33, *KJV*.
11. Quoted by Joseph N. Bell in *Kicking the Youth Kick* (Chicago: The Blue Cross Association, 1970).
12. Quoted in *The Generation in the Middle* (Chicago: The Blue Cross Association, 1970).
13. Philippians 3:13,14, *TLB*.
14. See Hebrews 12:15.
15. Psalm 91:1–5, *TLB*.
16. *Time* (August 6, 1973), p. 61.

4.

Enthusiasm Is Never Out of Date

How's your posture?

Posture is "body language," and if the Holy Spirit lives inside us believers, certainly our whole person—body, soul and spirit—should reflect the radiant fact of His presence. When Queen Elizabeth of England is in residence at one of her castles, the sovereign's flag is run up the pole over the castle so everyone will know Her Majesty is inside.

Why shouldn't our physical bearing and countenance and personality announce *who* is inside? Christians should be "up" people. They're the only ones in the world with "Good News!" they should be the eternal optimists—and look it.

Anne: *Ray came straight into marriage from the Navy, and one of his first husbandly commands to me was, "Woman, suck in your guts!" I had been very carefully raised, and it was one of the first of a million adjustments on the way to happy oneness.*

But the truth was I needed reminders about posture; and pretty soon, because Ray was being taught of the Lord and from His Word, he gave me the same message from Psalm 3:3, "Thou, O Lord, art ... the lifter up of mine head!" (KJV). *Now and then through the years, as we're walking along, Ray will gently run his finger down my back and quote to me Psalm 3:3.*

Let's take a good, long, encouraging look at vitality and enthusiasm for life from God's point of view.

The word "enthusiasm " actually comes from two Greek words *en* and *theos: en* meaning in and *theos* being the word of God. So enthusiasm is actually derived from the state of being *in God!* Full of God, and living in God's fullness! This puts a completely new light on things.

You may have become so sophisticated that you think enthusiasm is something out of date. Oh, no! You desperately need enthusiasm. Without it life is poor; with it life is good.

The enthusiast in the true, original, bedrock sense of the word, draws from deep resources. He is "in God." Those deep, deep wells are equal to any problem he'll ever have to face.

That doesn't mean you won't fail sometimes. But Charles F. Kettering, who used to be chief research scientist for General Motors Corporation, used to talk about *how* a man fails. The enthusiast "fails forward"! Thomas Edison would come to the dinner table many times after one more experiment failure and say with great encouragement, "I now know one more way that it can't be done!"

David sang in a psalm, "I will never lay aside your laws, for you have used them to restore my joy and health."[1]

The Bible is full of stories of people who lived "in God" and were vibrant until the day they died. Take Caleb. "As you see," he says, indicating that it was apparent to everybody, "from [earlier days] until now

44

the Lord has kept me alive and well for all these forty-five years since crisscrossing the wilderness, and today I am eighty-five years old. I am as strong now as I was when Moses sent us on that journey, and I can still travel and fight as well as I could then!"[2] So he's pleading with Joshua to give him new territory to conquer; he doesn't want to stand still.

Listen, resurrection life within you is more actual energy than you have probably ever realized or utilized. Romans 8:11 in the *Phillips* translation says, "Nevertheless once the Spirit ... who raised Christ Jesus from the dead lives within you he will, by the same Spirit, bring to your whole being new strength and vitality."

Ray: *I think once we catch hold of the concept of ministry, so that we know what to do with our time, and our lives, then the Holy Spirit is free to pour energy into us. Many times Christians pray, "Lord, give me power!" and the Lord is saying, "Power for what?" He doesn't waste His energy.*

I am so grateful for men around me who are spiritual tigers. They've seen that, when all is said and done, all that matters is God, and people, and connecting the former with the latter—and that's what their lives are all about. That's "ministry"—whatever your job may be.

I think of my dear friend Ted, who has huge visions of all God will do through his life. He never mentions physical weaknesses, though he could; but he always has strength to do the Lord's business, and to seek to lead men to Christ. Inside of him, the Holy Spirit is that deep wellspring of motivating energy—and it puts a sparkle in his eyes and a hearty exhilaration, always ready for fun.

Now, after we've underscored and underlined this true, real wellspring of vitality, then it's time to say a few—a very few—words about care of the body. The psalmist prayed, "You made my body, Lord; now give me a sense to heed your laws."[3]

First, FOOD. Daniel 1:8–17 tells an interesting story about Daniel's determination to eat wholesome simple foods instead of the king's rich food and wines—with this meaningful result: "God gave [them] great ability to learn and they soon mastered all the literature and science of the time, and God gave to Daniel special ability in understanding."[4]

Prayer before eating should be more than a ritual; it should be a statement of obedience to God that we will eat what He wants us to eat, and the amount that He tells us! Sensitivity to His leading in this important area will have the direct result of increased awareness and vitality.

This doesn't mean you get picky! Don't go the routine of "I eat only two minute eggs" and "don't slice my meat too thin" and "send this soup back to the kitchen". An attitude of cheerfulness and gratitude will really aid digestion! As 1 Timothy 4:4 says, "For everything God made is good, and we may eat it gladly if we are thankful for it, and if we ask God to bless it, for it is made good by the Word of God and prayer" (*TLB*).

Our family spent a summer in England, and our three rules for the summer were, "Stand up straight! Watch your weight! Keenly appreciate!" (We didn't want to miss a thing!)

Parenthetically, gluttony is a terrible thing in a world where there is such dreadful hunger. Sensitivity here will surely cause us to eat with sincere gratitude and prayer for those who are hungry.

Second, EXERCISE. Says Bob Mockler, "Middle age is when you're not inclined to exercise anything but caution!"[5]

Anne: *For Ray, exercise is no problem. Ever since he shaped up for high school football and then college football, he's just never quit. He says running, calisthenics, and handball keep his mind alert hours longer at his desk.*

For me, it's hard work. Nobody could be less athletic than I am! But my 5'3½" 111-pound frame can't stand any extra flab, so—just for Ray—I do 10 to 15 minutes' worth of stretching, bending and workouts every morning, and have done so for more than two years now. I don't do it because I like it; I keep saying, "This is for you, Ray; this is for you." I guess, though, even I appreciate the results.

Senator William Proxmire, our famous jogger, says, "At 57, after eight years of hard, dedicated exercise and a deliberately limited diet that has reduced my weight, I find that I have far better endurance than I did in high school or college, and that I can run longer and farther without being tired."[6]

Use the stairs instead of the elevator; walk instead of ride; take the long way around. Keep at it. But remember, it's not the key to happiness!

Ray: *I often meet a fellow at the "Y" who is "Mr. Body Beautiful." He has the build of a Mr. America. But when I ask him how life is going, his answer is always, "It's the same old baloney."*

"Bodily exercise is all right, but spiritual exercise is much more important and is a tonic for all you do."[7]

So what gives you vitality?

1. *God* brings vitality to your life.

"He fills my life with good things! My youth is renewed like the eagle's!"[8]

2. *Wisdom and common sense* give vitality to life.

"Have two goals: wisdom—that is, knowing and doing right—and common sense. Don't let them slip away, for they fill you with living energy, and are a feather in your cap."[9]

3. *Godliness* brings vitality to your life.

"Blessed is the man who walks not in the counsel of the wicked, nor stands in the way of sinners, nor sits in the seat of scoffers; but his delight is in the law of the Lord, and on his law he meditates day and night. He is like a tree planted by streams of water, that yields its fruit in its season, and its leaf does not wither. In all that he does, he prospers."[10]

In other words, this "blessed person" isn't bothered by external circumstances, isn't worried by long months of economic depression or any other kind of outward scantiness. He lives on those deep, internal reserves—those springs of God within.

Ray: When I was in the Navy I had a black friend who everyone knew was a joyous Christian. One day the sea was rough, and walking across the ship's deck, he stumbled.

Somebody kidded, "Hey, what have you been drinking?"

His immediate reply was, "Livin' water, man, livin' water!"

4. *Waiting on the Lord* produces vitality.

"He gives power to the tired and worn out, and strength to the weak. Even the youths shall be exhausted, and the young men will all give up. But they that wait upon the Lord shall renew their strength. They shall mount up with wings like eagles; they shall run and not be weary; they shall walk and not faint."[11]

Friend, God does not faint or grow weary. And He is willing to transmit His strength to the weary of any age. The only qualification to receive it is to admit that you're weary, that you dare not depend on your own resources, and that you will wait on the Lord. Then you can both run and walk—whichever is called for—sometimes one, sometimes the other.

"Look to him, and be radiant!"[12]

Dr. Oswald Hoffman said on his "Lutheran Hour" broadcast, "What is old age, this thing that makes young people shudder and older people weep? When do we get old?

"I had a friend of 75 who never got old. He died eventually, but he never got old. He was always young—with young ideas, young ways of doing things, a youthful approach to all of life, always getting ready for tomorrow and looking forward with excitement to the day after tomorrow."[13]

That septuagenarian knows the real truth about life for the Christian: "All the sugar is at the bottom of the cup."

Footnotes

1. Psalm 119:93, *TLB*.
2. Joshua 14:10,11, *TLB*.
3. Psalm 119:73, *TLB*.
4. Daniel 1:17, *TLB*.
5. Quoted by Bob Goddard in St. Louis *Globe-Democrat*.
6. Senator William Proxmire, "How to Feel Better and Better as You Get Older!" *Family Circle* (August, 1973) p. 98.
7. 1 Timothy 4:8, *TLB*.
8. Psalm 103:5, *TLB*.
9. Proverbs 3:21,22, *TLB*.
10. Psalm 1:1–3, *RSV*.
11. Isaiah 40:29–31, *TLB*.
12. Psalm 34:5, *RSV*.
13. Dr. Oswald Hoffman, "Lutheran Hour" booklet.

5.

Make the Most of Now

The two of us were sitting one day in a restaurant when gradually we realized that another woman's voice was getting louder and louder. Soon everyone stopped talking, and we all heard her. Here came this loud voice: "*Now* is all you get. Don't expect tomorrow, forget the past. Now, N-O-W—that's all!"

Well, as Christians we know that people are eternal, and that "now" isn't all you get. But that's exactly why your life *now* is so important; you're preparing for forever!

We believe it was Amy Carmichael who said it so well: "We will have all eternity to celebrate the victories, but only a few hours before sunset to win them."

In this second half of life, let's get on with it! Let's get some white-hot desire for living well!

Ray: *There's an interesting thing I've learned from getting ready to preach. I must never save a fabulous illustration or truth for some other time, some more august occasion, some time in the future when I want to fire a big gun. Whatever subject I'm preaching on, I must tell the highest and best truths about it, everything I know on the subject, and use the best possible illustrations—even if I'm speaking to a gathering in somebody's living room. If I hold back anything for some future date, I break faith with that present opportunity.*

I have to trust the Lord for tomorrow's manna, tomorrow. But it's "now" I've got to give life all I have.

The same is true in sports. I have to play my best at any given moment. I've always got to give my best shot right now—not wait for later.

Ephesians 5:15 and 16 tells us to "redeem the time." What on earth does that mean? Well, picture a bargain hunter who's just gone through the newspaper ads to see what the best buys are. The newspaper is under his arm. He's going around to the stores, looking in the windows; he's looking for bargains.

That's it! Christian, you may have wasted time up to this point, but the issue is *now*. Buy up every opportunity you can, *now*. Go hard after God, *now*. Invest where it's safe, *now*.

Even Jesus, given about three years' career time on earth, felt this urgency. "I must work the works of him that sent me," He said, "while it is day: the night cometh, when no man can work."[1]

Dad, when you have the attention of that son or daughter, and you've got 20 minutes alone—that's a bargain. Buy it!

God's moments for witnessing come when certain people will listen, when individuals were never as open as at that moment. That's a bargain. You sense it. Buy it! "Redeem the time."

There's a time when a nation is open as never before. We seem to be in that day. Never in our memory, at least, has it been so easy to speak about faith in Jesus. That's a bargain. Jesus called it harvesttime. "The harvest is plentiful, but the laborers are few; pray therefore the Lord of the harvest to send out laborers."[2]

Anne: *In our neighborhood things are really opening up. Ours is not a coffeeing, in-and-out-of-back-door neighborhood. The large, detached homes set in their own grounds mean that you can go for years with only a fleeting glimpse of a neighbor. Trouble brought the first one to open up her heart to the Lord. When we began having weekly Bible study together, a second one from across the street joined us—and she and her husband both wonderfully accepted Christ, and he's in a small prayer group of men with Ray. Then another neighbor from down the street joined our Bible study and reactivated her Christian faith. And throughout the area now there is a new buzzing about what's going on. At teas, at bridal showers, God is in the air. I tread softly, and ask God to use me in this "now" time to influence many lives for Him.*

Opportunity is never forever. Someone said, "Opportunity is like a horse that gallops up, and pauses for a moment. If you don't get on, before long you hear the clatter of hoofbeats dying away in the distance."

Ray: *A team of us was ministering recently on a college campus. At the first of the week I had the privilege of explaining that this was a special time that God had given us all; that back home, Lake Avenue Church people were praying for us around the clock; that there was a mighty force of God at work among them; and that very seldom did they get the privilege of stopping and spending extra time together looking at God, and getting hearts and relationships restored. I said, "This is your time." And they bought it.*

The first night some 30 students came by the microphone and said they'd wronged other students or faculty in some area, or they said, "I want you to know I love

53

you" ... *lots of opportunities were bought up. And all during the next day this kind of thing was going on; students using that special time to get right with God and with each other.*

That next night 300 of the girls met together with Anne in a large lounge, spilling out into the hallway, until one o'clock in the morning. They bought up opportunities to share their deep longings and their needs, and they cared and prayed, and they loved each other in the Lord.

On the final night the "team" decided that we should pull away and allow the Dean of Students to communicate with the kids by himself. They were "his people." We went to a hotel near the airport so we could catch a plane the next day. At 11 o'clock that night the dean phoned us and said, "Ray, heaven's come down, and glory has filled this campus." He said, "When I gave opportunity before the Communion for the students to praise God for something He'd done in their lives this week, 150 walked by the microphone one at a time, sharing various things they were saying God had done for them."

They had opportunities; they bought them—rich, precious experiences, which can never be reclaimed.

These beautiful moments are not just for the young. Paul, in Ephesians 5:16 tells you to redeem *your* time, whoever you are—and especially if part of your time has already passed!

That's a strong word, that word "redeem." It doesn't mean, "Stay out of trouble." It doesn't mean, "Don't take any wooden nickels." It means, "Be aggressive in the business of life for God."

In 1848, John Ruskin wrote to his father, "If one were to calculate average life at 80, I am now at noon, you at six in the evening; with both of us, the day is far spent.

I never think of my day's work much after 12, and yet I fear (forgive me if I am wrong) that neither of us have either chosen our master or begun our work."

Here's an out-and-out warning to anyone who thinks he's gone into a "holding pattern." There *is* no holding pattern! You're dipping, and it takes you about 10 years to find out that you've dipped and you're not what you once were. You've started to coast. And when you start doing that, you start to vegetate, spiritually.

Anne: *I must confess that when I look at Ray, often I think how precious this time is—these years we have together. When he proposed to me, he used the words of Psalm 34:3: "O magnify the Lord with me, and let us exalt his name together" (KJV). That motto hangs over my desk to remind me constantly what our two lives are for, and I have a great fear of living less than that—of going into spiritual decline and uselessness.*

Nevertheless, I know that that's what our two lives are for, separately as well; and if God ever parts us, we're still committed to magnifying Him with every precious moment of "now," one moment at a time.

Ray: *It takes re-commitment to the Lord, over and over and over. There's a downward drag inside of each one of us—inside me. I can start to get critical, or no fun or just lazy and procrastinating. I can start getting softer, more self-centered: you know, "Eat, drink, and be merry, for tomorrow we diet!" I can start excusing myself too much. It's easy in my life-style to say "no" to something which ought to be highest priority, because I say I don't have time.*

Ernest Dimnet asks some questions that help us all face the time problem more squarely: "Have you really no time? Are you sincere, or are you just repeating what everybody else is saying? No time! The extremity of poverty!

"Have you learned how not to give in to idlers? Can you steel yourself against the temptation to give pleasure to people whose laziness needs no assistance? Do you discriminate between kindness and weakness, never refusing to do a good turn, but always refusing to be a dupe? Are you an absolute slave to the telephone?"[3]

Strip down, friend. Get tough with yourself. Soft Christianity is the laughingstock of hell! Redeem the time. Buy up every opportunity for your life. The great apostle Paul, right to the very end of life, was crying out to God, "Oh, that I might get to know Thee, and the power of Thy resurrection, and the fellowship of Thy suffering, that I might be conformable unto Thy death!"[4]

Ray: *For me, discipline has to take many forms. It means being tough with things I once tolerated. Lots of things pressure me to get done, and I must continually say "yes" to God and "no" to lesser things; "yes" to my personal daily quiet time before I see people or answer letters or do administrative business; "yes" to workouts at the "Y" and "no" to too many desserts; "yes" to what will keep me centered on God, and "no" to what will diffuse me and scatter my shots.*

Many of these decisions are made behind the scenes, where nobody knows but the Lord and me. But for a disciplined life, I must have committed brothers around me in small groups, who will pray me through my weaknesses, as I do for them. It's imperative for me to ask them to hold me accountable, and to check up on me from time to time. Then I really begin to see the highest dreams for my life realized!

And it's always too soon to quit. Friend, there's always an opportunity waiting for you. An immigrant was coming from Europe to America, and his ship was wrecked. He was floundering out in the water, and he grabbed a piece of log and yelled to another fellow, "Which way is America?" That's the spirit.

In this period of your life, what are the "now" things you need to do? For the two of us, one thing is to write this book. So far there are three Ray-books published, and one Anne-book,[5] but this is our first together-book. We couldn't have written it earlier; we didn't know enough. We dare not write it later when we can't. So other things must be put aside.

This fifty-first year of our lives—this is it! We've been gathering material for a year. We've used part of a summer vacation to get a running start. We're working part-time on it this fall, winter and spring; then next summer's vacation, and our deadline is September first. This book is our "now" thing.

What's yours? What should you do "now"?

You say you have 70 years to get it all done. You really have nothing of the kind.

What did you know about life up to age five? Not much. So let's subtract those years. That leaves 65.

But you sleep 25 years or so—so you have only 40 years.

Some years are spent in rest and recreation; some years may be spent in wickedness . . . .

How much is left? Not much!

And how much total time will you have for your life, anyway? If you're between 35 and 50, you're doing well. Keats died at 26; Shelley at 30; Schubert at 31; Alexander the Great at 33; Mozart at 35.

On the other hand, it's never too late to start living. Michelangelo began building St. Peter's Cathedral at 76.

Verdi was nearly 70 when he composed his "Te Deum." Grandma Moses started painting when she was 78. Tennyson was writing his greatest lines at 83!

The thing is, have you gotten going yet in life? If not, why not now?

Chapter 3 of Hebrews tells you to be aggressive, to *believe* what you're reading in this book, to be full of faith and hope—if "now" is going to make any difference in your life. Hebrews 3:7 is a powerful plea: "The Holy Spirit says, 'Today if you hear His voice, do not harden your hearts, as when they [the Israelites] provoked Me, as in the day of trial in the wilderness" (*NASB*).

Remember, the Israelites in the wilderness lost the sense of the presence of God. Consequently they forgot His goodness, forgot that He was committed to them. So they began to grumble and find fault, and they were miserable. God gave them quail; then He gave them manna, then water—all supernaturally—and yet they murmured and complained. They were not in a believing condition.[6]

Now, they could have praised Him all the way through the wilderness experience; they could have rejoiced in Him. But their attitude disqualified them from all the blessings God was ready to give them.

We see the same situation in Luke 9. Jesus called three men to the great privilege of following Him. One said, "Yes." Two others disqualified themselves because they didn't have faith to believe that Jesus was followable and that His demands were right. Christian, believe that God has a good plan for you life! It will keep you pliable and optimistic. The Israelites forgot that, and became cynical and full of fears.

We read in Hebrews 3:8 that unbelief made the Israelites discouraging to others as well. And verse 13: "But encourage one another day after day, as long as it is still called 'Today,' lest any of you be hardened by the deceitfulness of sin (*NASB*).

If you're a believing person, you're encouraging to others. With a stance of faith, you're a help to those you meet. That's why your attitude toward the present is so important. Then you begin to be a power for God, a lifter, an encourager.

Ray: *I looked at my wife the other day when we were on a plane. She said, "Why are you looking at me like that?" I don't know what was on my face, but something was. I had just said a couple of things to her that had little barbs in them, and I thought to myself, "Ray, you're a fool! She's your friend. You don't tear up your friend that way; you love her and encourage her. You help her and lift her."*

I was saying to myself how sorry I was, and when she said that to me, I told her so. And in that moment God helped me switch from "un-faith" to faith, and I became an encourager. Now, I didn't have to switch to faith, but God helped me. Maybe somebody was praying for me right then!

Anne: *I'm tempted to tell something on Ray right here. It was a beautiful little incident—the other day he was down at the beach. (He gets such great thoughts at the beach, he really needs to spend more time there!) But he had two large problems—two enormous problems he didn't know how to handle.*

He told me he was walking up and down the beach praying, and the Lord said to him, "Why don't you thank Me for those problems? Why don't you have an attitude of faith toward them?" (We have a dear friend who often says, "Lord, allow me the luxury of watching you work!") Ray said, *"Lord, allow me the luxury of watching you work out these problems. Lord, I'm just going to look at you, and praise you. I thank you for these problems, because now I get to see you work."*

Ray says at that moment God gave him the privilege of having an attitude of faith, of believing God. It was a special time.

Now, is your appointed time to live, to care, to love. So how do you get moving? How do you really reorganize to savor each moment?

First of all, you've got to prune your life. There is much to get rid of! *The Los Angeles Times* writer, Charles Champlin, says, "In art, less is more. What is true can always be simply said."

In your life, too, as a Christian, less is more! The breathless, overscheduled person is underproductive, constantly apologizing for being late, not doing what he promised to do, and feeling guilty.

God is never in a hurry. To get the most out of life, to be mature, put every activity on trial.

How do you do that? "Less is more." Remember, we said you have to say "no" to lesser things so that you can say "yes" to greater things.

After this chapter is the time to take yourself to the mountains, the beach, the desert, somewhere away, to spend a good part of a day setting life goals.

Take paper, take your Bible, take your datebook or calendar; maybe take a hymnal. Maybe you'll even take a wife, husband, or friend, and do this together.

Ray: *When Anne and I take ourselves away for a "Think Day" we often spend the first part of the time in worship and confession. We may go apart for awhile or not, but the point is to get our hearts right with God and with each other first. Then we're ready for the day's business with God: setting goals, reshaping our schedules, or whatever.*

When you go apart to pray over life goals, put three columns on a piece of paper. First put down your dreams—the things you long to be or do in this next segment of your life.

Then in another column write down, "What I've been doing that I know God wants me to quit." Probably some of them are excellent; they've been right until now. But now the good must be put away in order to do the better.

Write in a third column those things you're undecided about. You can think and pray about them more; God will give wisdom. But remember Jesus' words, "Anyone who lets himself be distracted from the work I plan for him is not fit for the Kingdom of God."[7]

Our friend Dimnet writes, "Our mind ... is like our eye: it must be single. Children, plain people, saintly people, artists, all people possessed of a mastering purpose leaving no room for inferior occupations, reformers, apostles, leaders, or aristocrats of all kinds, strike us by the directness of their intellectual vision."[8]

God wants you to have a life that is stimulating, that is powerful, that really makes a mark for Him. You can, you can! He doesn't want to waste anything he has made. He wants you to be able to say when you get to the end of life, "Bless God, I was helped on to the end. I didn't die before I was dead!"

Jonathan Edwards said, "I am resolved that while I live, I shall live with all my might!"

As you're alone with God and your three columns, see how your schedule must conform to your new sense of God's will for you. Put in the priority items; cancel

61

what has to go. Write your letters of apology kindly, but immediately and decisively.

Eliminate and concentrate!

Friend, later may be too late. Have faith in God's power to live *now* in you. Remember Paul's statement in Galatians 2:20 (paraphrased), "The life which I *now* live, I live by the faith of the Son of God, who loved me and gave Himself for me."

But you must start with the faith-life—personally, definitely, decisively. If you are not yet truly in God's family, come to Christ! Decide that you are going to live in the "now" with God. Now is the acceptable time!

Paul pleads to the Corinthians, "As God's partners we beg you not to toss aside this marvelous message of God's great kindness. For God says, 'Your cry came to me at a favorable time, when the doors of welcome were wide open. I helped you on a day when salvation was being offered.' Right now God is ready to welcome you. Today he is ready to save you."[9]

Now God is dealing with you, as you read this. *Now* Jesus stands at your door and knocks and says, "If anyone hears me calling him and opens the door, I will come in."[10] "There is *now* no condemnation awaiting those who belong to Jesus Christ."[11] Decide *today* whom you will obey.

There is a story of the demons in hell having a strategy session, deciding the best way they knew to thwart the work of Christ in the world. The winner said this: "Tell the people to decide tomorrow. Tomorrow will be soon enough."

Footnotes

1. John 9:4, *KJV.*
2. Matthew 9:37,38, *RSV.*

3. Ernest Dimnet, *The Art of Thinking* (Greenwich, Conn.: Fawcett Publishing, 1971), pp. 104, 105.

4. See Philippians 3:10.

5. Ray-books are *Reach for Life; Lord, Make My Life a Miracle* and *Lord, Make My Life Count.* The Anne-book is *Up with Worship.* All are published by the Regal Books Division of G/L Publications, Glendale, California.

6. See Exodus 16 and 17.

7. Luke 9:62, *TLB.*

8. Dimnet, *The Art of Thinking,* p. 55.

9. 2 Corinthians 6:1,2, *TLB.*

10. Revelation 3:20, *TLB.*

11. Romans 8:1, *TLB,* italics added.

6.

Positioned for the Future

"N. W. Freeman, Board Chairman of Tenneco Inc., looks out on the skyscrapered Houston skyline, then looks you square in the eye. 'We're positioned for the future,' he says."[1]

When Freeman talks like this he is thinking future. God expects His people to think future—to be "positioned for the future." That's why He spoke to Joshua and said, "You are growing old ... and there are still many nations to be conquered."[2]

"Still many nations ... ?" Think about your life; what still remains to be conquered? How can you be "positioned for the future"?

They say about age groups, "Youth looks ahead; old age looks back; middle age looks worried!"

But youth has no monopoly on forward vision. Middle age can look ahead, too. Think what an exciting gift God has given you—one precious lifetime! So Proverbs 27:12 says, "A sensible man watches for problems ahead and prepares to meet them. The simpleton never looks, and suffers the consequences" (*TLB*).

Since God has specific plans for you, therefore it follows that you need to lay out your life, guided by Him, to fit in with those plans.

"We should make plans," says Proverbs 16:9, "counting on God to direct us" (*TLB*).

Those last six words about God's direction are crucial. "Seekest thou great things for thyself?" said Jeremiah; "seek them not."[3] The emphasis was on the words, "for thyself." Jesus said, "Lay not up *for yourselves* treasures upon earth."[4] A self-centered life is never lived to the glory of God!

Ask God, right at the outset of our talking about human planning, to purify your motives.

Now we're ready. Why don't we do more winning in this game of living? It's amazing to discover that the reason is because we don't make full use of that invisible but indispensable key to living well—foresight.

What about you? Have you deliberately stretched your imagination to project, as best you can, what's probably coming in your life? Only then will you know clearly what to do and what not to do. You'll be "positioned for the future."

Let's start on a small scale. What's coming tomorrow, or three days from now? That will determine today.

Anne: *At bedtime every evening I spend five minutes at my desk looking over tomorrow's list of things to do. Pencil in hand, I scan my datebook for the coming week: "Friday night is an important event; I must send my dress to the cleaners tomorrow morning. Thursday I have an appointment for which I need to gather information tomorrow to be ready."*

Being ready! That's the key! I must cut to a minimum the times I'm taken by surprise. I can pretty well predict what is coming; it's a matter of being ready.

Then when I know what I'm going to do tomorrow, I'll know what I need to wear. I check it over so I'm ready to fall into it quickly in the morning.

I can't tell you how much it's helped me to train myself to think ahead! I have a spot—my dresser—where I put Tomorrow's List. Then beside it I put Tomorrow's Things. (The book I'm returning to a friend because I'm having coffee with her; the brass piece I'm taking to have refinished because it's on the way to where I'm having coffee.) I put together Tomorrow's List, Tomorrow's Things, and Tomorrow's Clothes. Then I wake up "tomorrow" ready for the day.

You say that it doesn't seem orderly to have things piled like that? Well, that way I find I have a more orderly mind, a more orderly life, and I save time and confusion because I'm not forgetting things, backtracking, apologizing and retracing my steps as much as before. Each day is full and busy, but I feel more on top of it all, instead of life being on top of me.

But then, after the List, the Things, the Clothes gathered the night before, begin the day with prayer.

Ray: *I like to start out the morning covering my whole day by prayer. After a time of praise and confession, I take out my appointment book and pray through the hours. I pray for everyone I am scheduled to see. I ask that I may be helpful to them, but also open to what they may have for me. I pray for the unscheduled ones I will bump into. I've found that if I pray over my interruptions and get them squarely under God's sovereign control, they don't irritate me. I realize that they are part of God's plan.*

So pray over your day. Pray about every phone conversation; pray about your lunchtime. The lunch hours are important to use for God. Pray over evening; pray and think about the time you'll be with those you love the most.

Pray through your day before you experience it. Then relax. Whatever comes—you've got it covered.

Now you're ready for the day. And the year. And the second half of your life. Jesus, "who is made unto us wisdom, " says in Proverbs 9:11, "I . . . will make the hours of your day more profitable and the years of your life more fruitful" (*TLB*).

Think of your life also in chunks of weeks. As you look over the week ahead, prepare not only by doing, but by refraining from doing. Do you have a weekend coming which will be emotionally draining? Ease up beforehand; block out time to recuperate afterward.

What's coming? Think future! Be ready!

Much of the fear of old age is a subconscious feeling of panic, "It mustn't happen yet; I'm not ready!" Well, just as you sit down at your desk each evening to plan tomorrow, plan two quiet times during the course of reading this book: one, to sit down with your loved one for a half-day or a day to plan for at least the next section of your life; and two, to have an appointment with God about whether you're spiritually ready. No child of God should live as those "who through fear of death have been living all their lives as slaves to constant dread."[5]

First, the nitty-gritty. What are your plans in case of sudden sickness? What are your plans in the event of failing health? Don't live in your big house until you're too weak to move! Visualize the future; move while you can do it. Always be ready for the next day, the next season, the next phase of life as it will probably be.

Someone has said, "A good beginning is half the battle." And a wonderfully wise man wrote, "Any enterprise is built by wise planning, becomes strong through common sense, and profits wonderfully by keeping abreast of the facts."[6]

Being "positioned for the future" also means being ready for the inevitability of death. Jesus, during His earthly life, was always positioned for the future. He saw each phase that was coming and got ready for it. He explained patiently and thoroughly to His disciples about His approaching death and resurrection, so they wouldn't be caught off guard. And He was willing to submit to the entire experience because He was thinking future, "Who for the joy that was set before him endured the cross, despising the shame...."[7]

How do the two of us stay ready for death? Well, we try to stay caught up on all the things we want to have done by the time we die. The disease of procrastination adds terribly to the fear of death because there are all those things you haven't done yet, so you just mustn't go because you're not ready!

Anne: *Ray was attending the Congress on World Evangelization in Switzerland and had left me home to categorize all our gathered material on this book.*

There I sat, piles of paper all around me. Nels had gone to camp for a week, and I was reveling in solitude and uninterrupted concentration.

"How do the two of us stay ready for death?" I wrote, stringing together our collected ideas. "Well, we try to stay caught up on all the things we want to have done by the time we die...."

I put down my pencil and got up from my paper piles. I phoned for two filing cabinets to be delivered to the basement. I got out shoe boxes and cartons, all the old receipts and cancelled checks of 15 years of living in this house, and filed them in order. (No, you don't need that many years back for income tax, but you do for capital gains tax when you move.) I entered all the "house improvements" in a new red "house notebook." And I threw out all those dusty old cartons and shoe boxes.

Then with the same "house notebook" in hand, I went from room to room listing every possession, with original cost, as best I could, and approximate age. (I discovered our home insurance was low.) I marked beside the valuables which child should get what some day. (My mother had done that, and what a relief to her children.)

When the red notebook was complete with improvements lists and possessions lists, and the file cabinets held our financial history, then I went back to my paper piles and started writing again: "The disease of procrastination adds terribly to the fear of death, because there are all those things you haven't done yet...."

If I think of anything more we may not get the book finished, but we'll surely be ready to die.

Now the spiritual preparation! Without that, mere paper work means very little. It's not considered sophisticated taste anymore to ask, "Brother, are you ready?" But—"Brother, *are* you ready?"

This preparation need not take sitting down at your desk in the evening, or arranging a day together with your loved one; God is so available! Right now, give Him your heart. Accept the forgiveness of all your sins which He offers you through the death and resurrection of His Son, Jesus Christ, and you can know right now you are ready for heaven. If this idea needs amplifying, read the Gospel of John, and go to a friend who knows Jesus Christ to help you find Him, too.

But for the great majority who read this book who are already in the family of God—you're wholly washed, but have your feet gotten dirty along the way? Are there any you need to apologize to? Are you keeping short accounts with God, telling Him as He makes you aware of sin, that you're sorry? Day by day stay ready to die.

Some wise person said, "When you go to die, make sure that all you have to do is die!"

For the Christian, there's absolutely nothing morbid about the thought of death. On the contrary, it's getting ready to go visit your very best friend. And since you haven't been notified of the exact day of departure, you just stay "caught up" in the happy anticipation that today may be the day. Fabulous!

As John wrote, "And now, my little children, stay in happy fellowship with the Lord [that much is our year's verse for this year] so that when he comes you will be sure that all is well, and will not have to be ashamed and shrink back from meeting him."[8]

There's a story about a fellow left blind by some mysterious eye disease. One day while lying on the living room couch, he became aware of a light bulb nearby. Then he began to see shapes around the room.

With his heart pounding, he called to his wife in the kitchen, "Honey! Come quick! I can see!"

From the kitchen came this panicky voice: "Oh, dear —don't look now—I'm a mess!"

There are both practical and spiritual things you can do right now so that you're not caught a mess, and you can live in joyous anticipation of the Big Day.

Good living makes good dying!

Stay "positioned for the future," all your life.

Footnotes

1. Chris Barnett, *Flightime*, July '74.
2. Joshua 13:1, *TLB.*
3. Jeremiah 45:5, *KJV.*
4. Matthew 6:19, *KJV*, italics added
5. Hebrews 2:15, *TLB.*
6. Proverbs 24:3,4, *TLB.*
7. Hebrews 12:2, *RSV.*
8. 1 John 2:28, *TLB.*

7.

Set Goals
to Choose the Best

Barbara Fried, author of *The Middle Age Crisis*, says that facing the second half of life is an exhilarating thing to do. She writes, "It is only the truly mature who are old enough to know, young enough to do, and capable enough to manage the burdens of authority. Thus, middle age should be regarded as a time of accomplishment and rewards, of early ambitions fulfilled, of involvement with a world for which we have, in our turn, become responsible.... In short, these have to be the prime years of our lives."[1]

And yet, plenty of those supposedly in their prime are feeling panicky and unprepared for the present, much less the future. Life is passing by and they have the increasing feeling they haven't found the handles with which to grab hold of life. They haven't assessed where they are, so they don't know where they're going. Dr. Karl Menninger, president of the Menninger Foundation in Topeka, Kansas, says that most of these people are too busy to think about their goals. They're too pressured and overwhelmed by the demands of every day to consider where they're going and where they've been.

"Perhaps it's only in the late middle years that the

lack of a clear sense of direction and the absence of specific goals become an appalling reality," says Dr. Menninger. "Many persons reach that point in life with a bitter sense of loss and regret, wondering where time and opportunity have gone."[2]

As Dr. Menninger says, the very fact that the middle years are usually the busiest years can be our undoing. Not that these years are filled with great productivity; they're simply the years when old activities haven't been abandoned, but new ones have been taken on, until every day is clogged with unrelated duties and clutter. We heard a middle-aged friend say recently, "I never do anything, but I never sit down."

For a moment you won't think this next story has any connection, but listen. A very gentle, loving young man we know arrived unannounced at a lady's house, and she came to the door with her hair "teased" in six million directions. There was nothing for her to do but comment, so she said, "How do you like my hair?" Soberly, graciously he replied, "It looks as if it's just about to become something great."

So you, poised on the edge of facing the second half of life, may feel as though your whole life-style at the moment looks like teased hair. But settle down, keep reading, and maybe it's just about to turn into something great.

Let's think about what you're doing with your time. Right off, realize that you have all the time you want for everything you need. The reason we can say that is perfectly clear: God created time, and God created you. Then He put the two of you together. If you think you don't have enough time, it's because you're doing things He never meant for you to do.

Busy, creative, fulfilled people always have enough time, because they have limited what they want to do, and they're going after only what they've decided to go after.

You really have much more time than you think. You can recoup it from inferior movies, empty talk, magazines which don't contribute much, dawdling.

"But," says the flesh, "I've worked hard all day. *I owe it to myself.*" But when you've dawdled or chattered idly, do you really feel refreshed and restored? No? Then you used the time poorly. Saying "no" to the lesser and "yes" to the better will revive you and cheer you and make you ready for work again.

Anne: *My Bible and my notebook are never away from my side. Then if I have a delay, I'm rich with ways to fill the time! I read through the Bible each year, so maybe my need (at that moment of delay) is to get out my pencil and read.*

One of my goals is to pray over my goals three times weekly—!—and to pray for each member of my "small groups" of prayer and commitment three times weekly; so I may open my notebook and pray over goals or people. Or I may use "Acts" for a prayer time right in my head: A, adoration; C, confession; T, thanksgiving; and S, supplication.

I find that I welcome delays as times to get my spirit back together again!

What time of day is your peak energy time? Block it out every day for what is most important to you. Reading, meditation, prayer—one hour well spent when you're at your best is worth two spent earlier or later.

Proverbs 21:5 turns out to be so true: "Steady plodding brings prosperity" (*TLB*) to the mind and heart. And this very interesting observation, Proverbs 10:27: "Reverence for God adds hours to each day" (*TLB*).

Hard work never hurt anybody. It's only a bad attitude toward work that debilitates. How does God want you to serve Him? What are your gifts? Is your highest obedience to His will to teach, to count money, to hire and fire, to run an elevator, to preach, to fix cars? It may be any of these things—but think about your job in the light of eternity. God will not say to you on that great Judgment Day, "So you became vice president of your company! My, I'm impressed. What did you say that salary was, again?"

How, through your gifts, can you best elevate God? How can you best serve and help His people? How can you do His work in this world? The point is to see what He's given you to do, and settle down and do it.

By middle life if we're still dazzled by a multitude of "things," we'll only be followers forever—one minute charmed by this, another minute by that—with no clear sense of direction and purpose. Of course, we have sloughed off many things we don't have the talent to do, many things we're not interested in. But we still haven't learned the art of specialization. Life is passing by and precious hours every day are spent in worthless ways: newspaper reading, television watching, conversations with people—none of which add to our specialties.

Decide what you want to go after, then really seek it. Narrow your interests. What pursuits give you, under obedience to God, a sense of achievement and satisfaction and contribution? Then concentrate on those few things. Specialize! Say "no" to many things, in order to say "yes" to a few. Eliminate and concentrate!

Robert Louis Stevenson said, "The world is so full of a number of things, I'm sure we should all be as happy as kings!"[3]

Don't starve within an inch of plenty! Reach out!

One of our datebooks has at the bottom of a page, "Be

76

satisfied with God; be satisfied with life; but don't be satisfied with yourself."

The two of us have notebooks which, among other things, include personal goals. First, after much reflection and prayer about five years ago, we made lifetime goals. (These may well change. At this point they haven't.) These are mainly visible, measurable goals.

(Now we are really becoming "open books!") Here is a sampling of Ray-goals, listed under "Priority One":

1. *Begin each day with my first thoughts of God, and first words to Him.*

2. *Have a quiet time daily and worship God.*

3. *Have a day of prayer and planning each month.*

There are other goals. These are some listed under "Priority Two":

1. *Have prayer and fun times with my family regularly; save all Mondays for this.*

2. *Speak well of the church, Christ's Body, to my family and friends; write three notes of thanks or encouragement to Christians each week.*

3. *Be in three supportive fellowship and discipleship groups.*

4. *Pray for and encourage the church staff daily.*

There are more! Under "Priority Three":

1. *Pray daily for a contact with a non-Christian to speak to about Christ.*

2. *Plan with God for the outworking of Acts 1:8 in my personal life.*

There are still others.

Some Anne-goals are:

1. *To see all four children spiritually settled and fruitful.* (Three down and one to go on that one. Nels is 10 and coming along.)

2. *To write three books, each of which will aid the Body of Christ.* (One down and two to go.)

3. *To write five really successful songs which will greatly bless the church.* (One down and four to go there.)

4. *To serve God together with Ray until we're at least 85, seeing Acts 1:8 fulfilled abundantly.*

Then after we have set down life goals, *out of those* we make one-year goals. You see, the coming year is a chunk of your life and if you can see a bit of your life goals accomplished in this coming year, you'll start to say, "Hey, I think I'm going to make it! With God's help, I'm going to win!"

"It's hard
 By the yard,
 But a cinch
 By the inch!"

Out of our one-year goals we make three-month goals.

Ray: *For instance, because of "Priority Two, number three (about being in groups), one of my goals right now is to get up a good plan for the new small groups I'll be in in the fall.*

Anne: *And because of my lifetime "children" goal, one of my current three-month goals is to study and pray with Nels daily.*

I'm "thinking future" when I do what I do. The chunks of my present life must be building blocks.

The basic unit of our life is our week. We include here the outline we think is helpful to fill in before a week begins.

What do we want to see happen in this coming week? We jot in the goals on the left—our dreams, our wishes in black and white—what would make it a very fine

78

week! Then we block in the prime times when goals will be made to happen.

Next, we fill in other meetings and appointments already scheduled. Some of these take preparation time. So we note this on the left and then fill in when the preparation will take place.

We also fill in rest times and fun times with loved ones! Then when something less important comes up we can honestly say, "Sorry, we're already booked!"

Have you done this? We recommend it!

When you've finished reading this chapter, sit down in quiet thought with your calendar. When can you get away for the better part of a day to set your sights for your lifetime? If you're too busy for this, friend, you're too busy! Set a time when you can ask yourself, thoughtfully before God, "Where am I going? What do I want to give myself to?"

Anne: *I was teaching a Bible class the other day, and God taught me while I was speaking. I'd never thought of it this way before, but the words came right out of my mouth:*

"Your visible life should be only the tip of the iceberg —or at least just the top part of a ship. If you shot out of bed this morning and your entire day was spent in visibility, you're as unstable as a ship would be with no keel underwater.

"The greater the proportion of your day—of your life —spent hidden in quiet, in reflection, in prayer, in scheduling, in preparation, the greater will be the effectiveness of the part of your life that shows."

And in the meantime, practice right now. Using the chart on the next page as a pattern, take a piece of paper and make a few goals for the next seven days. How can

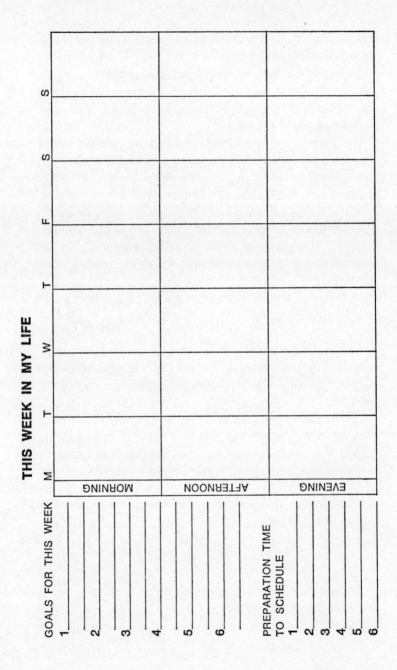

THIS WEEK IN MY LIFE

GOALS FOR THIS WEEK

1 _____
2 _____
3 _____
4 _____
5 _____
6 _____
_____

PREPARATION TIME
TO SCHEDULE

1 _____
2 _____
3 _____
4 _____
5 _____
6 _____

	M	T	W	T	F	S	S
MORNING							
AFTERNOON							
EVENING							

this coming week, this first piece of your exciting future, be lived wisely and well?

Put down the place in each day where you're going to cause your goals to happen. Those are the priority spots! If it's quiet time with God, make it at your own "top energy" time; make it at a realistic spot in the day when it can really happen; and make it long enough for your personal needs. (Ten minutes or two hours, only you can know.)

What needs to be eliminated? You must learn to *save yourself for the best.*

If a day's trip means a second day to recuperate, it may no longer be best for you.

If an hour's tennis drains your strength for the next half day, it may no longer be best for you.

Plan your day around (as you will plan your life around) giving yourself to the best. Then let your moderate diversions be the stimuli to bring you quickly back to the best again.

Set your goals. Then let your life revolve around those.

Here are two of God's promises from *The Living Bible:*

Psalm 23:3, "He helps me do what honors Him the most."

Psalm 25:12, "Where is the man who fears the Lord? God will teach him how to choose the best."

Footnotes

1. Barbara Fried, *The Middle-Age Crisis* (New York: Harper & Row 1967), quoted in "The Meaning of Maturity," *The Generation in the Middle* (Chicago: Blue Cross Association, 1970), p. 96.
2. *Time* (August 6, 1973), p. 61.
3. Robert Louis Stevenson, *A Child's Garden of Verses* (New York: Rand McNally & Company, 1902), p. 55.

8.

By Ray,
on His Fiftieth Birthday

Laguna Niguel, California
2:00 A.M., July 10, 1973

It's been my birthday today. Fifty years old! I've been working today at bringing my "Ugh, I'm half a century old" to "Praise God, I'm 50!"

Friends from Afghanistan have been visiting us for a few days, and I suggested this morning that Anne and Nels take them to Disneyland for the day. I would spend my fiftieth birthday alone with God and good reading.

It's been a wonderful day to think. Except for the waitress at the restaurant where I went for dinner alone, I haven't talked to a single human being all day long. I spent sections of the day in various mental disciplines: really studying the formation of the trees around me, the clouds, the beach, and praising God for what I was, reviewing all I could remember of my first 50 years of living, and praising God for all His input into my life. I walked, I jogged, I did calisthenics.

Now at the end of the day I'm writing memoirs of the day (waiting for that ridiculous family of mine to get in from Disneyland!). I reviewed today how God by His sovereign grace caused me to be born in the United States of America. I'm grateful. And He placed me in a

Christian home, with stable people who were physically and mentally and spiritually sound. I had no say about all this! It was God's doing.

The day was spent reviewing and planning.

What do I need to cut out of an overstuffed life that makes my days so fat I can't get to my goals? Who are the people I should be with? Who are they who do not need me, whose lives I only complicate as they do mine?

What do you do when you are 50? I don't feel old; I'm in good shape. I run two miles a day and I can beat most of the "young bucks" around in handball.

But face it, Ortlund: You're 50. You're well into middle age. Realize it; look at it.

First of all, as I look I see that I'm in God's sovereign hands. He is the One who strongly started the universe and who is "working all things after the counsel of His own will" (see Heb. 13:21). Time is not important to Him; a thousand years are as a day, and a day as a thousand years. He can pack an eternity of events into a brief hour. Ortlund, get off the old-age kick!

Second, I want to seek the will of God for *now*, and for the next few years. I don't want to make retirement the big thing. I want to give life a whirl now. I want to go for broke!

How may I best love and lead my family?

How many can I win and disciple in the next five years? Who are they, and where are they? How do I carve out the hours this winning and discipling will take? What method should I use to bring a non-Christian to Christ and then on to maturity? How do I maintain my own spiritual vigor, while giving myself to others?

Fifty years has given me a chance to accumulate tons of trivia. I need to pare down at 50. I need to lose weight; weight around the middle, weight of unimportant associations, weight of unimportant activities. I see from

Hebrews 12:1 (*KJV*) the command to "lay aside every weight" as well as "the sin which doth so easily beset"; the love of ease and comfort I can tell myself I deserve.

Fifty years old. I'm both at my best and my most dangerous time of life. To grow at 50 will take courage and discipline. The world hurts; it needs love from Jesus, and practical help, too. There are believers who hurt and who need encouragement.

You're 50, brother. You only get one whack at life, and yours is going fast. Give it all you can—for Jesus' sake.

At this point in my reflections, still waiting for my Disneyland revelers, I created and went through a worship service, with the following notes:

Romans 11:33–36
Hymn: "O, the Deep, Deep Love of Jesus"
Doxology: burst of blessing
   God's depth of riches;
   God's depth of wisdom;
   God's depth of knowledge.
God . . . is deeply, enormously rich, wise, and knowledgeable.
   No one knows His mind or counsels Him.
   No one can give a gift to God; all comes from God in the first place.
   All comes from, through, to. (That's a full circle.)
   Glory to God!
Man . . . is incomplete, dependent.
The world . . . is of God and for God.
I must depend for all from God, and join in giving Him glory.
From 50 on, what matters?
1. Worship
   Get identity: God is, and I am in God.

Realize true purpose of life: for God.
2. Purity
No place for "dirty old man" mentality.
Hebrews 12:14,15. Holiness with happiness.
Continual battle.
3. Relationships
Mounting number of relationships tend to confuse, diffuse;
  I can hide behind knowing many and not really be known by anyone in particular.
"Christian jet set"—not where true action is.
Family
Friends: love all, know a few well.
4. Thinking
I ought to be learning how ...
Not just rearranging my prejudices.
Takes concentration on fewer things.
What do I need to do in the next 15 years?
What do I want to do?
  a. To know God
  b. To excel in helping others know God:
  Family
  Small groups
  Lake Avenue Church congregation
  Congregation at large: preaching and writing
For these I must stick to priorities:
  Study continually how to reach priorities
  Rise early (no more reading in bed at night)
  Use every time-saver possible.

At this point the family arrived home. Praise God, hugs, and off to sleep.

9.

Anne's Thoughts on Being Fifty

I wish I had something authentic, like Ray's, written on my fiftieth birthday. I never thought of it! I can't even remember what I did. Ray always takes me out on a date for my birthday, but often we can't celebrate on the exact day because of board and committee meetings and all the rest. So it must have been like my other birthdays: Somewhere within the week there was a dinner out for the two of us, and tender words, and so on; and on the very day, loving cards and presents from the children.

Anyway, what's the big deal about turning 50? I can truly say I've publicly announced being 27, 34, 41, 48, 50. It's my age. It goes with me like my red hair, green eyes and 111 pounds. In fact, I confess that when I see other women fearful of age, I enjoy mine all the more (and dear God, you know the fine distinction between victory and pride).

Come to me next year and I'll tell you I'm 51, and 10 years from now I'll tell you I'm 60. So I've got bifocals; I sure wouldn't trade them for pimples and braces. God's gift of time is so wonderful. How else could we ever progress toward heaven?

There's that great verse, Romans 12:2, "Be not conformed to this world ..." (*KJV*). Only the Western youth cult has made us reticent about our age. We're supposed to be Bunnies forever—vacant minds and all! What a drag, to have your life cave in when you see a double chin appear! Really, is that the mentality we women want?

That beautiful lady of Proverbs 31:25, "shall rejoice in time to come" (*KJV*); she "smiles at the future" (*NASB*). In other words, she aggressively looks forward to future days with happy anticipation. It's part of her "positive thinking." It actually makes her prettier because it puts the lines on her face in the right places!

But in my heart I do have a fear. I confess it. I long to grow more godly with each passing day. Call it "the fear of the Lord," being in awe of Him and scared to death of any sin that would mar my life at this point. With a clear conscience I want to live through my last years and rush straight into the arms of Jesus, joyous all the way. Not "laughing all the way" as in "Jingle Bells," but in the deep delight of living in God. There's no delight like that!

There's another fear which many have that I confess I don't. They say, "I don't mind the goodies of growing older (like freedom from raising children and more independence), but I fear pain and I fear sagging skin; I fear possible disease, or senility...."

Well, let me use an illustration. Ray and I have parented four children, each one so precious to us. What if one of our children said, "I don't mind the goodies of being your child (food, housing, clothes, allowance). I just don't want the going to school, the homework, the chores around the house; and I don't want you to tell me what to do...."

We'd answer, "It's all part of the package, kid! You get the good news, you get the bad news. Earth is now, heaven is later. Expecting heaven now is pure escape!

For now you need the homework and chores and discipline to shape you into that wonderful, mature adult we look forward to enjoying later on.

"But in the meantime, understand that we won't try to lay it on too heavy. We don't want to 'provoke you to wrath.' We study each of you carefully and try to give you enough pressure to make you grow strong, but not enough to crush you and defeat you.

"Fair enough? Are you willing to stick it out with us?"

Success will come if your children trust your competence as parents. Then they'll be willing to stick it out.

And success for you and me through every stage of life will come if we trust the competence of our Heavenly Parent. If we understand that He really loves us, we can relax.

I look for enough "bad news" to make me grow strong and ready for heaven, but never enough to crush or defeat me. That's the life of faith.

In the meantime, away with negative fears, apprehensions, and all the "what if's!"

I see from God's Word how the godly turn out, and I want to be one of those: "The godly shall flourish like palm trees, and grow tall as the cedars of Lebanon. For they are transplanted into the Lord's own garden, and are under his personal care. Even in old age they will still produce fruit and be vital and green. This honors the Lord, and exhibits his faithful care" (Ps. 92:12–15, TLB).

I read that and say, "Why shouldn't I be a great advertisement of the Lord's care at age 50 or beyond? Any kid can look all right when he's four; he just got here. I want to go through 50 and come out looking great—an exhibition to all that God takes wonderful care of His own."

Final thought on the subject: Age doesn't matter unless you're cheese.

Middle Time

Between the exhilaration of Beginning
and the satisfaction of Concluding
is the Middle Time
   of enduring, changing, trying,
    despairing, continuing, becoming.

Jesus Christ was the man of God's Middle Time
between Creation and . . . Accomplishment.
Through him God said of Creation,
"Without mistake."
And of Accomplishment,
"Without doubt."

And we in our Middle Times
   of wondering, waiting, hurrying,
    hesitating, regretting, revising;
We who have begun many things—
and seen but few completed;
We who are becoming more—and less;
through the evidence of God's Middle Time
have a stabilizing hint
   that we are not mistakes,

that we are irreplaceable,
that our Being is of interest
and our Doing is of purpose,
that our Being and our Doing
are surrounded by AMEN.

Jesus Christ is the Completer
of unfinished people
with unfinished work
in unfinished times.

May he keep us from sinking, ceasing,
wasting, solidifying—
that we may be for him
experimenters, enablers, encouragers,
and associates in Accomplishment.

—Lona Fowler

Lona Fowler, *Activity* magazine, published by the Congregational Board of Evangelism, Volume 6, 1968.

10.

Marriage in the Middle Years

An old lady tottered into a lawyer's office and asked for help in arranging for a divorce. The lawyer just didn't believe it. "Tell me," he said. "How old are you?"

"Eighty-four," she said. "And my husband is 87."

"How long have you been married?"

"Almost 62 years."

The lawyer slapped his forehead. "Married 62 years? Why do you want to divorce now?"

"Because," she said, "enough is enough."

Unfortunately, multitudes of married people get to that "enough is enough" point long before 84.

A while back a housewife wrote "Dear Abby":

"I wonder what has happened to our marriage? My husband doesn't even seem to enjoy the meals I prepare for him any more, and I'm told I'm a 'fabulous' cook.

"We've been married 25 years, are both young and healthy, and don't look our ages.

"Do all marriages go sour after 25 years? He doesn't have anything to talk to me about any more. I have no major complaints, but that old excitement is gone. . . ."[1]

Someone has written, "By middle age the fires have been banked, but the glow and warmth of the fire is even more comforting than the tempestuous flames that consumed a couple in the earlier years. The physical union of a man and woman during this period is equally re-warding, but it is different. It is this difference that every middle-aged man and woman needs to accept."

What is this difference?

The difference is that both you and your partner now have less energy. Why?

For one thing, your bodies are that much older than when you started marriage. But factors other than age can also drain your energy. And involvement is one. Both partners are more involved in life around them, which is draining both psychologically and physically.

Boredom itself can increase fatigue and sap energy. So you need to ask yourselves: Are we genuinely excited about God and about life?

Yet what remains unchanged at this time?

You always need affection! But your children are probably teenagers now who are too preoccupied to give you as much affection as they did when they were young. Or they have left home and there is no one else around to give you that affection—except your marriage partner.

The problem is, most married couples' expression of love decreases with the years, and fewer demonstrations of affection and tenderness cause sex to be devitalized.

Says Richard Halverson, "Then comes the strange appetite.... Some try working harder, getting busi-er.... Some drink more, but that isn't the answer. Some get involved in extracurricular activities—club, golf, trap shooting, etc. Another seeks satisfaction in ex-tramarital adventures. Convention time is play-around-with-women time. He tries to prove he's still a man, still attractive, still a 'lady-killer.' The kickback is worse than the hunger."[2]

It's always worth remembering that *the sexual joy of any couple can rarely transcend the general level of satis-*

faction that a husband and wife have with each other.

That makes us stop right here and now and say this about our own marriage: We've gotten past many a rocky place along the way by constantly affirming one another. The words have to continually flow:

"Honey, I looked at all those women in the group there tonight, and none of them looked as good as you."

"Darling, I had no idea when I first said 'yes' to you, that I was getting such a winner."

And the flow must go on and on, day after day, because we know that if it slows to a trickle, we're going to be in trouble.

Adam *knew* his wife, says Genesis 4:1, and we find that sex is more than functional; it must be communal. It's not that the man is relieved of something, but that he gives something. It's that the woman receives joyously, and, in so doing, gives back.

And the back-forth flow goes on through words, forever and forever. Then the conversations become just as tender, just as sacramental. They are prelude, they are postlude.

We love each other.

What happens to communication in marriage? Do a flashback. You fell in love. You fell out of circulation. It was great! You had private communication: you developed "our mountain," "our song," "our joke."

Life was very specialized, with its special language! But life was probably limited to dates, and to "up" times when you looked your best, talked your best and romanticized with sentiments far more luxurious than you could afford.

Then you married and, unknowingly, revised your communication. Marriage was real. It was 24 hours a day, and busy with meals, budgets and lawns. There wasn't any more time for "our song." In the light of daily problems the words of love seemed silly.

Disenchantment was a shock, and you lacked maturity to accept each other *as you really were.* Probably communication got departmentalized. Romance, formerly the big scene, become 20 minutes in bed once in a while. The rest of the time, you were wrestling with life. And your roles began to diverge and there was less to talk about.

Anne: I got my eyes open to one of my special booby traps when I saw what was happening to me through the eyes of a team of researchers, Robert O. Blood and Donald M. Wolfe, both of the University of Michigan, who concluded this about wives in the middle time: "The wife, now freed from the cares and concerns of child raising, uses the time and energy to increase her power in relationship to her husband."[3]

They backed up their statement with their findings in critical research:

Husband's power, on a scale of 0–6:

During honeymoon:	5.35
Preschool:	5.11
Preadolescent:	5.41
Adolescent:	5.06
Postparental:	4.79
Retired:	4.44[4]

The wife domination takes over, as the children withdraw, in ever-increasing strength and self-confidence! She's gotten to the point in life where her skills are sharpened, her opinions are molded, she's more sure of herself. And if the kids aren't there to tell off, father is.

It scared me to death. I went back to those beautiful words in 1 Peter 3, and I prayed, "Lord, give me the beauty of a meek and quiet spirit, which in your sight is of great price."[5]

I'm not there yet, but this is a specific prayer request of mine to my close sisters, and God is helping me.

You remember in Shakespeare's Taming of the Shrew, *what Kate finally learned to say:*

"Why should our bodies soft and weak and smooth,
Unapt to toil and trouble in the world,
But that our soft conditions and our hearts
Should well agree with our external parts?"

Who hasn't seen a woman soft and feminine on the outside, and tough and crude and rough and rude on the inside? I have no desire to be strident-voiced and demanding in this world. I don't believe that is God's way of making wrongs into rights. I have no desire to run parallel to Ray, sprinting down the track in competition. I want to be behind him, encouraging him, being strong where he is weak just as he is strong where I am weak—making out of both of us what we could never be alone.

All of us married people have to realize that time is a corrosive influence. We don't naturally drift closer together; we drift further apart. We have to fight our way back to each other, day after day, year after year, as long as we live. Across the board, in marriages that survive, the evidence seems to be that in every succeeding decade of the average marriage, the partners are less satisfied with each other and with their marriage! They no longer talk as much, interact as much. Strangers under the same roof, they live in increasing loneliness. Yet both have needs for love as great as ever—maybe greater.

But, praise God, we see lots of married couples around us who, like ourselves, are more in love, more fulfilled, more crazy about each other than they've ever been; and we know that there is this kind of marriage all around the world, too.

The two of us can look right into each other's eyes and sing, "I get no kicks from champagne (don't even touch it), but I get a kick out of you." We wouldn't dare write this book together, otherwise.

It hasn't always been easy. The thing we've got going for us has been forged and beaten out of controversy and joys and tears and fun and total misunderstandings and having a ball together. We still have irritations around the edges, and we always will, because the edges keep shifting! But the big, main hunk of our marriage is solidly in cement. You better believe it!

And there is a sense in which every time the authentic Word is proclaimed, the Word must be made flesh—backed up by a sincere attempt at obedience. If our mouths are open, our lives had better be open, too—open books, "epistles read of all men."

So what are we suggesting, you two Christian people, to put sizzle back into your marriage?

1. Hope. That must come first. A great marriage in the second half of life isn't a fuzzy pink cloud that isn't there when you reach for it; it *is* there for you. We know because ours is a great marriage.

Don't put down this book if your marriage is just on the toleration level. Pull those dreams out of your memory; all the things you longed for when love was new. Are they still available?

It all depends on how big your God is. Marriage is *His* invention, and He planned it for you long ago. Perhaps He planned that at this very time in your lives you'd come back and try it *His* way, and turn a new corner in your lives together.

You look in a mirror, and you say it's too late? Ridiculous! "Never forget," says an old philosopher friend of ours, "no matter how old you are you can still be somebody's dreamboat—even if your anchor is dragging and your cargo has shifted." One of the beautiful things about the second half of life is that there starts to be more emphasis on wisdom and less on the physique; more on know-how and less on first appearances. And this shift in emphasis benefits every area of your life, including marriage.

Consider this philosophy: Some societies allow polygamy—one husband being married to a number of wives. However, we say that in our culture we practice polygamy in a new form—one husband (wife) being married to many wives (husbands), but one at a time, through divorce and remarriage, divorce and remarriage. This system has a very strong argument in its favor: We change constantly throughout our lives, and —at any given point—we are not the same persons our partners married.

It's true!

So the two of us endorse a form of this system: Do get married, over and over through your life—but always to the same person. You have changed; she has changed. Recommit yourself to this changed person. Keep your present married status fresh and new.

Ray: *Every now and then I end a sermon on marriage with a rededication of those couples present by going through the ceremony again. There we are: the church, the organ, witness of friends—and children, the rings and a ready kiss.*

But it's interesting to watch the expression on the face of the fellow who's lost the joy of marriage. He's the reluctant groom! And he's caught in front of all those people saying lines which are sticking in his throat.

As I write this I'm thinking of the other night when I did this in San Diego. After it all, a middle-aged couple came up hand in hand with tears still glistening, saying,

"We can't thank you enough. This has brought a new start to us." Their pastor said to me, "They mean it. They've been through a terrible time."

2. *Discover renewed companionship during this period.* Let the weaning away of your children from your emotional lives drive you two together again; deliberately seek each other. Go off on a honeymoon. At least increase your date life—just the two of you.

Talk! It will be embarrassing, but so it was when you got acquainted the first time. When you're faced with something hard, you can't solve it by running away or pretending it isn't there. You have to plow right on through it until you come out the other side. But take it easy. Don't "talk problems" all the time. Have fun too.

Ray: *Not every issue needs to be settled. Once in a while we have an honest disagreement. Anne has a mind of her own, and that's one of the things I liked about her from the start, but it's also been hard for me to accept at times. I must have strong feelings of my own; because I can remember once, after I'd given the obvious, conclusive remark to end all discussion with our older son, his return was, "The wisdom of the universe has spoken." Ouch!*

I've learned that the best way to take the sting out of differences is to say, "Darling, I don't agree with you, but I respect your opinion, and I love you." That's a lot better than getting so frustrated you throw an empty Coke bottle down on your beautiful dark-stained hardwood floor. I did that once in our home in New York, and I had to look at the scar on the floor for the remaining years until we moved out of the house.

Anyway, why do we have to agree, or win, or conclude

every discussion? Some great truths are opposites, and must forever be held in tension.

3. *Discover how you can share more tasks, intermingle your roles, achieve new intimacy.* We discovered that we could spend a whole day together speed-reading for sermon material; and we do, out of town in some secluded spot, every Thursday of our lives! It's work-oriented romance. It's hearts-and-flowers in pragmatic form. Someone we know had this to say, "I saw us walking hand in hand through life, but now it's clear all we really need is two cars." (We don't agree with this.)

4. *Develop new relationships with other people.* Tenderness and "with-ness" cannot be demanded from grown children. (We must hasten to add—because our grown children will be reading this book—when you back away from them, amazingly enough, they often come freely for companionship. And how sweet it is!)

Deliberately glean new companions from among your own peers. Develop a "ministry." Have fellowship in depth. Meet the needs of others; in so doing, your own needs will be met. Serve in the church; give your gifts freely, together.

Ray: *Anne and I have committed ourselves to Christ and then to the Body of Christ, in that order. This second commitment takes on reality in our "supportive fellowship" group, a company of committed couples to whom we are accountable. There is a tendency sometimes to elevate the pastor and his wife so high they can't breathe; this "supportive fellowship" group remedies that! In that small circle of dear friends, the "stuff of life" gets out in the open, and we are prayed for and loved.*

I meet with several discipleship groups of men, as well, and I couldn't imagine ministering without these. But when Anne and I are in a group together, that's refreshing in its own special way.

5. *Discover the joy of intellectual searching.* Read broadly and well. Make time to study the Bible together as a couple and with other couples, so that your minds grow together and you meet your friends at a high, cleansing level of communication.

"Man is the only creature," someone has said, "that is given the power to make choices, to improve thus upon yesterday, and to level the road for tomorrow. Days for men and women do not have to be the same; they can be full of innovation and exhilaration."

Anne: *Yes! I buy that all the way. Recently Ray and I met for lunch in a little restaurant and talked busily and incessantly for awhile about conference speaking dates, about music writing, about manuscript due dates and church affairs....*

Suddenly Ray's face had the look on it of "enough is enough." He leaned across the table and looked at me with his blue eyes, and he said, "Anne, I want to remind you of something, and don't you ever forget it. This isn't a working partnership. This is a romance."

Footnotes

1. "Dear Abby," Chicago Tribune-New York News Syndicate, 220 E. 42nd Street, New York, New York 10017. Used by permission.
2. Richard C. Halverson: *Perspective*, Vol. XXV, No. 44, October 31, 1973.
3. Robert O. Blood and Donald M. Wolfe, *Husbands and Wives* (New York: Free Press, Division of Macmillan Co., 1960).
4. Blood and Wolfe, *Husbands and Wives.*
5. See 1 Peter 3:4, *KJV.*

11.

About Your Money

Richard Armour writes this poem about money in his book, *Going Like Sixty:*

"Workers earn it,
Spendthrifts burn it,
Bankers lend it,
Women spend it,
Forgers fake it,
Taxes take it,
Dying leave it,
Heirs receive it,
Thrifty save it,
Misers crave it,
Robbers seize it,
Rich increase it,
Gamblers lose it....
I could use it."[1]

Well, money is important, for sure. God uses it to mold us and teach us about Himself, about power and authority, about submission and obedience—so many things.

The Bible is, among so many other things, certainly a money-management book. It tells you everything you need to know on how to get it, how to keep it, what to do with it. And most of all, it says that money is to glorify God.

So what is money really for?

First of all, it must be to glorify God. You must not glory in money itself. Rather, handle your money with the sure knowledge that He personally gave it to you, in the amount that He wanted you to have, to handle for Him.

Again, what is your money for?

To provide everything you need to live abundantly for Him. The last two words are utterly important: *for Him.* Every area of your life must be seen as contributing toward "ministry"; that is, being connected with God and connecting other people with God. If it's not, throw it out.

You can absolutely count on God to give you the type of clothing, house, life-style which is best suited to your particular ministry for Him. If you live your life as *ministry*—He won't skimp. And you'll have plenty, more and more, to give away.

And what else is your money for?

It's to see God's power and love in providing for you. "So don't worry at all about having enough food and clothing. Why be like the heathen? For they take pride in all these things and are deeply concerned about them. But your heavenly Father already knows perfectly well that you need them, and he will give them to you if you give him first place in your life and live as he wants you to."[2]

So, obviously, if you put God to the test concerning His promises, He can use physical resources to increase your faith and conquer your worry and bring you into a wonderful life of total dependence upon Him.

Like so many others, we have wonderful stories to tell of God's provision for us! Going to our first little church was a step *down* for us in income from our seminary days; can you believe it? And with three babies and a cold climate, soon the coal bill was out of hand.

One May we were really distressed. The bill was $367, and we didn't see any way to pay it before fall, when we would need to order more coal!

"Dear Lord," we prayed, "we've been faithful in tithing to you. Now it's your turn to come through."

So we got a letter in the mail from the State of Iowa! It had never happened before; it has never happened since. But it seemed there was a surplus in the treasury that year and they were sending each of their own veterans a check.

Ours was for $367.

What is your money for?

It's a way God directs and leads you. If you don't have money for a certain project, pray; if there's still no money, stop! God's telling you something. If there's money on hand, pray and proceed with caution.

What is your money for?

It's to unite in a wonderful way the family of God. Many times when we've read Acts 2:44,45, about the early Christians pooling their funds, we've laughed or tried to explain it away or hurried on to the next verse. We haven't known how to handle it. Personally, we're discovering in these exciting days of living in the Body of Christ how to love with our money, too.

Saying "I love you" to a fellow Christian is a beautiful and important thing to do—but slipping him money when he needs it certainly adds to the ring of authenticity. We're discovering these days that the Body of Christ caring for itself is more than keeping a supply in the Deacons' Fund for inner-church welfare needs. It means living closely enough to your brother that you're aware when he's caught between paydays, and you quietly do something about it. It has nothing to do with "I'm rich and you're poor." The Macedonians gave *out of their poverty.*

A couple we know whose total salary is $500 a month lovingly slips $10 sometimes to another couple in need.

Last year two of our parents died within four months, and suddenly we had big airline bills as a result of several trips to the East Coast from California. Unknown to us, our youngest married couples' class—many of them still in school—passed the hat and handed us $500. *Out of their poverty.* How we know they love us!

Whether you're midstream in the hassle of raising a family or past all that and into retirement, God will give you plenty of supply for *living for Him!* Believe that, live like it.

John Wesley gave interesting advice on money: "Earn all you can; save all you can; give all you can."

And God's Word gives you plenty of direction on how to handle the money that comes.

First, give! Give the first and the best. Let your gift to God be the first check written every payday, and give until you're a little breathless and dizzy; give through and beyond that pain threshhold to the place where, if He doesn't come through, you're sunk. Then you'll know the exhilaration of the faith-life—whatever your income base may be.

Anne: *Through the years as our "10 percent" has doubled and tripled and more, so has the excitement and the fun of risking and daring.*

Remembering that God talks about tithes "and offerings," one January first I told Him that in addition to our tithe checks, every time the offering plate passed, if I had a dollar bill I'd give it whether I thought I needed it or not.

That was such a good year, the next January first I said I'd put in two. Later on, one Sunday night I put in my last two dollar bills, knowing that the next morning before the banks were open, we had to go across Los Angeles to where we weren't known and take an Australian V.I.P. to breakfast. "Lord," I prayed, "please let Ray have breakfast money in his wallet."

Church ended; we shook the last hands and started across the now deserted parking lot. "Honey," I said, "I hope you have money for breakfast."

"No," he said, "I was so blessed, I put in my last five dollars."

Just then, lying on the parking lot pavement in front of us, all neatly folded up in a square, was a 10-dollar bill!

The next evening we happened to be taking Lorrayne, Ray's secretary, to dinner and we told her how God had fed our Australian breakfast that morning.

Lorrayne looked simply incredulous. "That was my 10 dollars!" she said." "It fell out of my shoe, and I almost cried. Then I asked the Lord to have someone who needed it find it."

(By this time we'd gotten more cash at the bank and we handed the 10 dollars back.)

Out of all the hundreds of people who had walked across the parking lot that night, God had ordained to let Lorrayne lend us 10 dollars for 24 hours—to increase both her faith and ours!

And the result of giving with risk? We didn't say this; Jesus did: "If you give, you will get! Your gift will return to you in full and overflowing measure, pressed down, shaken together to make room for more, and running over. Whatever measure you use to give—large or small —will be used to measure what is given back to you."[3]

What do you do next with the money that comes?

The second thing is to pay your bills. Proverbs 3:27, 28, says, "Don't withhold repayment of your debts. Don't say 'some other time,' if you can pay now" (*TLB*).

Watch those credit systems; use them only to establish good credit! Control your will-power if you have a tendency to run up debts. Ask your close brothers to pray with you about it, just as they pray over your taking off weight, or any other area where the loving watch of a fellow believer helps you be accountable.

Last summer our daughter, Sherry, and son-in-law, Walt asked if they could meet with us as a "small group." We had wonderful times in weekly prayer and fellowship together for those summer months.

Walt told us he'd made four vows to the Lord:

1. To have a daily quiet time;
2. To pray with Sherry every day;
3. To lose 15 pounds; and
4. To live without indebtedness, except his education debts to Uncle Sam—not easy when you're a seminary student with a wife, a baby and a BankAmericard.

A few weeks later he said to us, "You know, Mom and Dad, since I told my Thursday morning group of brothers about my vows, nobody has asked how I'm doing."

We said, "Tell them! They're not functioning,"

So the next Thursday morning Walt said, "Look, do you guys love me, or don't you? Nobody has asked me if I'm praying with Sherry, or if I'm into the refrigerator, or if I'm overspending. What's this group for, anyway?"

Well, the fellows really felt rebuked, and the next week the phone nearly rang off the hook as they were checking up on him.

And by September 15, Walt's goal date, he had lost 15 pounds; he had had a quiet time every day; he'd prayed every day with Sherry; and he was clear of bills.

You can have dinky little goals all by yourself—but if you want to be stretched to live a life of excellence for God, you need the Body of Christ close to help make it happen.

Know your budget. Spend or save with an eye on tomorrow, next week, next month. God will show you what to keep, what to give.

We heard about an old gentleman who said very cautiously, "When I were in school, they learned me figures, but not reading. So now when I sees a sign by the road, I can tell how fur, but not where to."

We want to know "how fur" we're going, and where we're going!

Your money is a crucial part of your total life before God. So listen carefully to these words of His for you: "Riches can disappear fast. . . so watch your business interests closely. Know the state of your flocks and your herds; then there will be lamb's wool enough for clothing, and goat's milk enough for food for all your household after the hay is harvested, and the new crop appears, and the mountain grasses are gathered in."[4] Rural terms—but the meaning is obvious!

What else do you do with your money?

Plan for the future. Make out your will—not just any will, a Christian will—tithe at least 10 percent of it to go to God's work after you're gone.

Don't put off making that will. A nationally known minister did just that and died intestate. He left his widow with a frozen bank account, no access to insurance papers, no money to pay bills, and years of unnecessary court proceedings. So plan ahead. Make your will now.

And keep your will up to date. When Bobby (Anne's brother), died in a plane crash at the age of 24, he left a 19-year-old widow and twin sons aged three weeks.

Yet somewhere in that three weeks, he had already made those little twins beneficiaries in his will—and everything was in order.

What more do you do with your money?

Most of all, transfer all ownership of it over to God. He's the wisest Financier! He can best show you how to conserve it, so that it can be the greatest blessing and return for your investment.

God's on your side! Relax. Surrender. Lay out the books before Him.

Footnotes

1. Richard Armour, *Going Like Sixty: A Lighthearted Look at the Later Years* (New York: McGraw-Hill Company, 1974), pp. 77,78.
2. Matthew 6:31–33, *TLB.*
3. Luke 6:38, *TLB.*
4. Proverbs 27:23–27, *TLB.*

12.

Stop, Look and Listen I

Americans are getting so wise to tourism that it's the "in" thing to abhor rushing from one European country to another, seeing too much, too fast. We used to come home exhausted and needing to "rest up from vacation." Now we're supposed to stay put longer, explore just a country or two in depth.

Yet the rest of the year when we're at home, we rush from one thing to another, skimming the top impression off each experience and then racing on to another.

For the 16 years we've lived in our present house we've had a tiny patio off the dining room that we've dreamed of improving: build a prettier wall to back it up, floor it with brick, add a tiny fountain and pool, a black wrought iron gate....

Why? Because it's gotten shabby. Because it would add to the value of the house. Because, as we occasionally eat in the dining room, we'd be aware of it, or as we race by through the house we'd give it a glance and enjoy it—like the tourist visiting the Louvre: "Quick, which way's the Mona Lisa? I'm double-parked!"

Anne: *Then Ray put a book in my hands: Ernest Dimnet's* The Art of Thinking. *Father Dimnet spends most of page 185 just describing his sensations as a little boy sitting beside the waterwheel of an old mill in rural France. You'd have to sit for a long time in quiet absorp-*

tion to describe this a half-lifetime later:

"*You went down and down ... at least thirty steps, the light growing stronger but of a strange green tint as you approached the bottom.... [There was] a deep cut through the polished slaty strata, [with] mosses and dainty ferns of all kinds hanging from every moist cranny.... On my right the broad wooden wheel seemed enormous and ferocious, and I would look away from it, knowing that I should be terrified if it should suddenly begin to turn and make its thumping noises while starting the stone and iron machinery upstairs. But ... the brook, broad and shallow, [caught] every green reflection from the walls and a little of the blue up above....*"

I have no such recollections—me, a city child, born running.

But I have a new goal in life. Before too many years, I want to be able to describe our dining patio from memory, inch by inch, color by color, sound by sound.

I want to build my patio with that in mind. It will be my dead-stop, thinking, discovery place. My retreat.

How about you? After having run through the first half of life, do you dare change pace? Join us. Deliberately cut down the overwhelming multi-media and multi-transport impressions seeking to engulf you. Your emotions can't handle being so bombarded, surfeited, overstimulated. Shut off the overproduction.

Thoreau said it eloquently: "Simplicity, simplicity!"

By a determined effort of the will, stop. Be quiet. See. Feel. Listen. Write in your notebook your descriptions, your impressions.

It's a delicious world. You know it so well from the window of a 747. But oh, have you examined it from the point of view of an inchworm?

112

13.

Stop, Look and Listen II

We were out together for a Thursday study day. "Plan A"—when the weather is good—is always the beach; we spread out the books all around us on the sand and pour over the subject for the day. "Plan B"—when it's chilly or rainy—is a hotel with a quiet nook! We know where plenty of them are in the Los Angeles area, and we sit among strangers and work undisturbed.

On this particular Thursday we were studying the subject of the Sabbath, and came upon a paragraph written in 1900 which sounded amazingly like today:

"It is not altogether that we work so much harder than our forefathers, but that there is so much more fret and chafe and worry in our lives. Competition is closer. Population is more crowded. Brains are keener and swifter in their motion. The resources of ingenuity and inventiveness, of creation and production, are more severely and constantly taxed. And the age seems so merciless and selfish! If a lonely spirit trips and falls, it is trodden down in a great onward rush, or left behind to its fate."[1]

We quit for a lunch break. Cigarette smoke drifted our way from the next table where a group of salesmen, with controlled, civilized decorum, were eating too fast, drinking too much, and subtly doing each other in.

And in that atmosphere we lost ourselves in another fabulous quote by F. B. Meyer, concluding his writings on God's Sabbath available to you and us. It's too good not to be included in this book as a key for getting ready to live the second—and best—half of life:

"When we learn to live by faith, believing that our Father loves us, and will not forget or forsake us, but is pledged to supply all our needs; when we acquire the holy habit of talking to Him about all, and handing over all to Him, at the moment that the tiniest shadow is cast upon the soul; when we accept insult, and annoyance, and interruption, coming to us from whatever quarter, as being His permission, and therefore as part of His dear will for us, then we have learned the secret of the eternal Sabbath of rest."[2]

Footnotes

1. F. B. Meyer, *The Way into the Holiest* (London: Lakeland Paperbacks, Marshall, Morgan & Scott, 1950), p. 55.
2. F. B. Meyer, *The Way into the Holiest*, p. 59.

14.

Extend Your Life

By now, perhaps, your mind is working in a few directions for reshaping the second half of your life, with all the right proportions of action and rest, thought, productivity and discipline. You've been praying about it, and God is shaping in your mind ideas that are right for you and that will bring credit and glory to Him. You're going to be a better advertisement of all that God can do for a person!

But is this going to be just for you alone? Is all this new wisdom for living going to be "the end of the line"? How many people do you dream could benefit by your life before God?

John A. Mackay, beloved to both of us as President for many years of Princeton Theological Seminary, spoke gorgeous words to our particular graduating class in June of 1950. We'll dip in and out and give you great sentences:

"The burden of my deep desire for you ... is this: *Keep moving beyond.*

"Beyondness is a unique dimension of the Christian religion. All the great Bible figures from Abraham to Saint Paul ... were not static ... nor complacent.... They soared, they ran, they walked.

"*Keep moving beyond the attainments of today....*

"Keep moving beyond the boundaries of tomorrow . . . Put the accent of eternity on everything you do. . . . Never let the local become the total. . . . Think of the folk beyond your boundaries; live with the far horizon in your eye."

Now, we are apt to think of those admonitions as a missionary challenge, if we're thinking in terms of space; and so they are. But also think in terms of time: How can you think of folk beyond the boundaries of your lifetime? How can you live with the far horizon of future time in your eye?

Jesus did. He had world evangelization in mind. His strategy was simply to pick a few men, and pour all His teaching and living into them. *But He picked men that the multitudes would follow*, after He was gone.

Anne: *Ray preached on this in January of 1974. He was talking about the need for each of us to be discipling others; and he told us, particularly us mature adults, "Don't huddle around with people your own age all the time and just fellowship with them! Then when you die, everything you know will die, too—because they'll be dying about the same time you do! Pour your knowledge into people 20 or 30 years younger than you. And when you're gone, everything you've taught them will be walking around this earth for another 20 or 30 years teaching others. Extend your life!"*

I was leaving the next week to speak at the Firs' Ski Chalet for a women's Bible conference. "What a beautiful idea!" I was thinking, suddenly so happy that most of my seven disciples were in their twenties and early thirties. So up I went to this conference—of Canadians and Americans, some urban, some rural, a beautiful mixture. Some had traveled 19 hours to get there from backwoods logging areas.

I repeated what Ray had just taught us about extending our lives. At the end of that particular talk, I saw two little ladies sitting on opposite ends of a long couch. I introduced myself to the first one, a thin, grey-haired lady whose eyes were glowing. She told me, "I've just discovered the reason I'm alive!"

Well, that sounded wonderful, so I asked her to explain. She said she lived on an island off the coast of Canada where their only contact with the outside world was a once-a-week ferry. There was one church there and she was the only old person in it; all the rest were young fishermen and their wives. She said she'd always been faithful to attend worship, but beyond that—the prayer meetings, the parties and the doings—she'd always said, "I'm just an old lady, you don't need me."

But she leaned toward me and said delightedly, "You know what? I've just learned that they need me!" She said she'd been raised on prophecy and the Scofield Bible and Keswick teaching and all these riches, and she was full of truths they didn't yet know. "But," she added, and I loved her for this, "you pray I won't come across too dogmatic and know-it-all; those young people know all this business about love and honesty, and I need to learn from them, too!"

Well, that was a thrill, and then I moved over to talk to the other little lady at the opposite end of the couch, also grey-haired. She looked grey in expression as well. She told me a few things about herself; that she lived on another Canadian island about half an hour by ferry from the other woman. Then she just said dully, "That was a nice talk, but it didn't any of it apply to me. I live alone. I've never married; I don't even have any real friends. I couldn't 'disciple' anybody."

My heart went out to her, and I said, "Tell me, what do you do for a living?"

You won't believe what she said: "I'm a house mother in an orphanage for Indian and Eskimo children."

I said, "My dear, there are all your built-in disciples!" I thought of the fact that she had told me she belonged to the Church of England, and I said, "With all the rich doctrine in that wonderful Book of Common Worship you have, you have so much to teach them! And long after you're gone from this earth, there will be hundreds of tall, beautiful Eskimos and Indians walking around Canada and Alaska filled with all the wonderful things about Jesus that they learned from you!"

She looked wistful. She said, "Oh, do you think I could? I do pray with each of them every night."

Then she looked discouraged. "But you said we needed somebody in the Body of Christ to pray with us and help us do it!"

At this point the other little lady reached her hand across the couch. "I will," she said. And before the conversations had ended, the two had arranged to come across the ferry once a week and have Bible study together and pray for each other and strengthen each other in God.

The whole conference was worth just seeing those two leave arm in arm, smiling and thrilled, ready to strategically "extend their lives," and help one another do it.

Friend, if you're 35 or older this is for you. It's God's plan. You see it from Genesis to Revelation, but think of a few particular spots:

In Numbers 14:29,30, God had told the Israelites that not any of them 20 years or older (except two) would get to enter the land of Canaan. Immediately, with chapter 15, God begins giving Moses instructions for those ages 19 and younger; Moses was to begin pouring the teaching on those precious teenage kids who were the future of Israel, and who would survive even Moses himself.

Even before this, Moses had picked one particular young man, Joshua, who looked especially promising, to be his personal disciple.[1] As you know, Joshua was God's choice, too; and after years of learning at Moses' side, he became his successor in leadership.

David was one of the greatest leaders of men. But never forget, he did not lead alone. The summary of his life includes the summary of his "band of men"—30 of them, and out of 30, particularly three.[2] They ate with him, fought with him, suffered with him, learned from him, and became wonderfully committed to him. For instance, Ittai once said, "I vow by God and by your own life that wherever you go, I will go, no matter what happens—whether it means life or death."[3]

Elijah had Elisha, a disciple so unusual that he received a double portion of the spirit of his discipler.

And so on, to Jesus Himself, who had the 120, and out of them the 70, and out of 70, 12, and out of 12, 3.

Now, this is not to say that you should invest yourself in just anyone. Before Jesus chose the inner core of His disciples, He spent a whole night in prayer.[4] And then, out of the multitude of His followers gathered there, He chose 12 men who had certain qualifications:

1. They were available. When Jesus said, "Follow Me," they did.

2. They were teachable. Sometimes they seemed to learn very slowly, but they stuck with Him and listened and asked questions.

3. They were men who had heart. How do you define that mysterious quality you sense in a person that says, "I want more of God in my life"? These men must have had that. Jesus never cast pearls before swine.

It's interesting that Jesus didn't pick Nicodemus. We

might have said, "What strategy! This man is a leader among the Pharisees, and he'll be our inroad into the religious movers of the day!" Nor did He choose Joseph of Arimathea, who could have financed their trips for the entire three years. Both of these men loved Jesus very much, and God was to use them in special ways at the end of Jesus' life. But perhaps Jesus knew that they were simply too enmeshed in the systems of their world; they weren't free enough to follow Him all the way.

Jesus chose disciples who were "loose" and available —but they were also men whom the multitudes would later follow. He knew they would not be the "end of the line." Paul told Timothy, also, to pick that kind of disciples: "You must teach others those things you and many others have heard me speak about. Teach these great truths to trustworthy men who will, in turn, pass them on to others."[5]

Invest truths not just to any younger Christians but to trustworthy ones!

We have learned that we must help disturbed people and those in trouble as we can. But we must not give the larger part of our time to them. We might temporarily help them, but they might never be strong enough to reinvest in spiritual children of their own "these great truths" we taught them.

Remember, Christ gave a lion's share of His time to those 12 men. And He did it because He could envision the whole book of Acts which was to follow! They were to be the foundation stones on which the whole church of Jesus Christ would be built. When you choose those whom you will teach, have in mind a great host of spiritual grandchildren.

Ray: *In my home church was a single lady, a graduate of Moody Bible Institute, who gave her life to the young people. She was not on the church staff; she simply had a heart for all of us. I think when she meets the Lord, He's going to give her a huge paycheck! She taught us the Bible, loved us, told us off and prayed for us constantly.*

She's an example of a single person who invested her life in those younger than herself, and so extended her life by perhaps 50 years. My listeners don't know it, but some of the things I preach are hers, too. Those listeners are not just in our congregation, but by radio across Southern California and overseas through the Far East Broadcast. The "great truths" that dear lady taught me are taken in by English-speaking people in the Philippines, in Vietnam, in Cambodia, India, Pakistan, East Africa and the Lord Himself knows where.

"Keep moving beyond . . . beyond the attainments of today . . . beyond the boundaries of tomorrow."

"Live with the far horizon in your eye."

Invest yourself in those who will invest themselves in others! Extend your life!

Footnotes

1. See Numbers 11:28.
2. See 2 Samuel 23:8–39.
3. 2 Samuel 15:21, *TLB.*
4. See Luke 6:12.
5. 2 Timothy 2:2, *TLB.*

15.

New Hope

When we started into Princeton Seminary with one and a half babies and little money, we rented the one-room attic of an old Pennsylvania farmhouse—with the privilege of sharing the bathroom on the floor below. It worked great: commuting time to the seminary was only an hour. And through the winter months we burned a light bulb every night under the old car's hood, so she started fine in the mornings.

It was fun for other reasons, too. We had little money, but no debts. College was at last behind us, and we were into the specific preparation for God's future. We loved each other. Sherry was our toy, and Baby Two was sturdily kicking.

Oh, yes, in that funny old farmhouse attic room, we were future-oriented for sure. The name of the town? New Hope!

It was a prosperous little hamlet, set in rolling, fertile land. You could imagine those early settlers who had driven their wagons into the area and staked their claims and were like us—future-oriented. "What shall we call this place?"

"New Hope! ..."

"That's it ... New Hope!"

Life was great for us there, and not just because we were 23. Life was great because there was the promise of so much ahead. We had wonderful *new hope.*

Regardless of your age, if you know the Lord and walk with Him, you can start in a new place (in your heart), orient yourself toward the future, and call it New Hope!

For you, Christian, every day of your life there's the promise of much ahead that's wonderful.

Periodically, in the years since New Hope, the two of us have come to a fresh "New Hope" in our lives. Like what we wrote down 13 years ago:

Ray's and Anne's New Points of Departure, May 7, 1962

1. New appreciation of all things and all people
2. Constant genuine joy of living by the Holy Spirit
3. Ten pounds off
4. New enthusiasm for each duty
5. More sporty dress
6. To bed by 10:00 P.M.
7. Together more for fun and reflection
8. Relaxation in the sovereignty of God, the cleansing of Christ, and the power of the Holy Spirit.

Those goals kept us pushing ahead for awhile. And there have been plenty of other points of departure since.

Now in 1976, as we sit beside the pool with this finished manuscript between us, there is also the awareness of much more between us: 30 years of tears, giggles, floor scrubbing, sermon preaching, hugs, crises, crazy darn fun, four great kids, high adventures and a great glob of stuff we've totally forgotten. Oh yes, there's much between us besides this manuscript.

"What shall we pray that God will do to the people who read this?"

"Well, that He'll give people heading into the middle of life renewed dreams and visions of what life ahead can be?"

"New Hope...?"

"New Hope! Do you remember New Hope?"

Do we! Attics and light bulbs and groping down a flight of stairs to the bathroom in the night.

Dear Father, New Hope was a great new beginning for us. Make this book a great new beginning for hundreds of thousands of your people.

In spite of their own versions of attics and light bulbs —whatever their struggles are—make them future-oriented.

Give them fresh starts.

Give them New Hope!

Epilogue

Well, look up from this book a minute. Who's that coming down the road toward you? It's you, 25 years from now. Oh, it's true, the outline of the figure is faintly shadowed. The blurring of your vision is simply your own heart saying, "If God wills. Lord, not my will, but yours be done—regarding death, illness, whatever your highest desire has planned for me."

But as best you can see through the mist, the approaching figure begins to look pretty good, right? You feel by now as if you know the Future You rather well; you could quickly sketch in your mind his or her accomplishments, life-style, temperament. And, God helping you, you pretty much like what you see.

Put down your book and glasses. The one coming toward you is no enemy, no ghost, no person to be dreaded or feared. Praise God, and put out your hand in sincere eagerness to the Future You. Welcome your friend. Accept your true comrade and ally.

And have some coffee together.